Dear Sarah Lee:
I hope you grow
up to be a *Just* wonderful
cook-- *Kidding!* just like your Mom!

Kid-friendly recipes for all occasions

+ we hope you make us every

meal in this book!

Lots of Love

Grammie +

Poppa

Christmas

2008

Simple Dream

D1298669

© 2007 Simple Dream Publishing
info@simpledream.ca

Original artwork © Joy Hall, licensed by Linda McDonald Inc., Charlotte, NC

Recipes : Joy Hall, Danielle Van Schaick, Christine L. Brière

Editor : Angela Rahaniotis

ISBN 978-1-897115-41-1

When I was about four years old, my father gave me a set of 12 colorful markers. I was thrilled with this wonderful gift. I recall spending many happy hours in the kitchen drawing and coloring with my new markers while my mother prepared the evening meal. Mom would take fresh vegetables from the refrigerator and place them on the table in front of me to draw. Even though I was too young to do very much actual cooking, she found a way to incorporate my love of art with her love of cooking for our family. This was a very special time for my Mom and me.

Cooking together can be a very rewarding experience for both you and your child when you find ways to make it fun. Involving them in the planning and preparation of meals will not only help them learn about food but also give them the opportunity to appreciate the process and work necessary. Allowing them to make decisions regarding menus will foster a sense of responsibility as well as a feeling of pride. But most of all, they will enjoy sharing this time with you.

★ ★ ★ ★ ★

The recipes in this book were specially selected for their kid-pleasing qualities and designed to provide a "fun" approach to cooking. With chapter themes such as Lunchbox Specials, Happy Birthday, and Pool Party and with playful illustrations enhancing every page, your kids will definitely be enticed to join you in the kitchen. The "Little Helper" is a charming character that appears throughout the book suggesting how your child can help out, with your supervision, of course.

● ● ● ● ●

Our philosophy in creating this cookbook: spending quality time with your kids: essential; inspiring recipe ideas for everyday meals and for special occasions throughout the year: valuable; creating some very special family memories: priceless.

-- Joy Hall --

Enjoy!

Contents

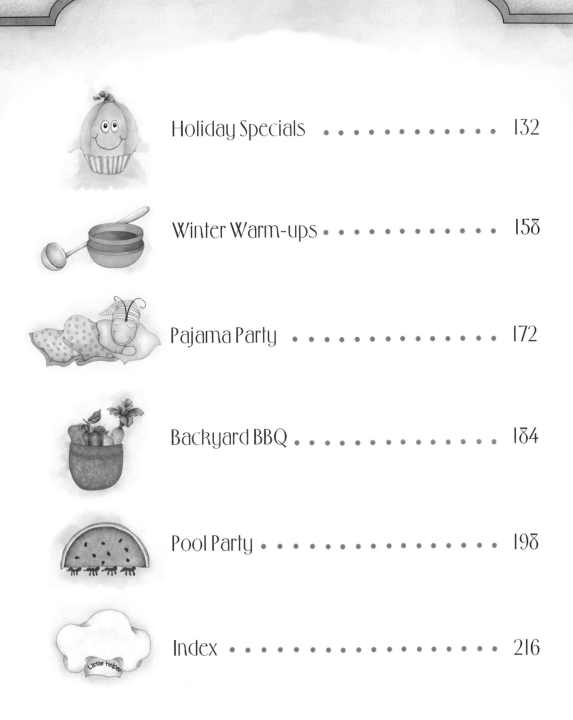

Breakfast is my favorite meal of the day. As a child, I loved waking up to the wonderful aromas that wafted from the kitchen, down the hall, and into my bedroom. Once I had kids of my own, I wanted to recreate the same wonderful morning experience for my family. I loved getting up early and heading for the kitchen to whip up both a nice, warm start to their day and also a nice, warm memory.

One fall morning, soon after my oldest son had begun kindergarten, I went to his school for my first parent-teacher conference. After his teacher had covered all of his academic highs and lows, she shared a little "Secret Sack" story with me. "Secret Sack" was an activity in which each child would bring something from home hidden in a small brown paper bag. In turn, they would each go to the front of the class and give clues as to what the mystery item was, while the other kids tried to guess.

On this particular occasion, a little girl had given a clue indicating how the hidden item (a whisk) was used: "Something your mother does when she makes pancakes." My son quickly spoke up and said, "Send you out of the kitchen?"

I immediately realized that I had missed the real secret of the "breakfast experience". I had been so focused on fixing the perfect breakfast that I had neglected to see what my son had really wanted: to share in the preparation. Have fun with your child trying the wonderful ideas for breakfast you will find in this chapter. In the process, you will share in creating many special memories.

Rise and Shine!

Breakfast Tacos

6 eggs
1 lb. sausage
1 onion, chopped
Grated cheese
3 baked potatoes
Pinch garlic powder
Flour tortillas

In a frying pan or skillet, scramble the eggs. Set aside.
In a separate skillet, crumble the sausage and cook until brown.
Mix in onion and grated cheese.
Add chopped (or grated) baked potatoes and garlic powder.
Cook on low heat for 5-9 minutes.
Add the scrambled eggs and cook an additional minute.
Warm the tortillas and fill with mixture. Serve immediately.

Serves 6

Spoon egg/sausage mixture on tortillas to make tacos.

Green Eggs and Ham

2 large eggs
½ tsp salt
¼ tsp ground black pepper
1 cup chopped fresh or frozen
   spinach
⅓ cup chopped flat-leaf parsley
3 green onions, green part only,
   chopped
½ cup chopped low-fat ham

In a mixing bowl, whisk together
the eggs, salt and pepper until
well combined.

Coat a medium non-stick skillet with cooking spray and heat it over medium-
high heat. Add the spinach. Stir in the parsley, green onions and ham. Cook until
the greens are wilted.

Pour in the beaten eggs and stir constantly until they are combined with the
other ingredients and scrambled.
Divide the cooked eggs between 2 plates and serve immediately.

Serves 2

Oh-So-Simple Crêpes & Waffles

3 large eggs
½ tsp salt
2 cups cold milk
4 tbsp butter, melted
2 cups all-purpose flour
4 tbsp sugar
Corn oil

In a large bowl, mix together eggs and salt. Stir in milk and butter; mix well to blend. Add flour and sugar and mix well.

Brush the bottom of a crêpe pan or heavy skillet lightly with corn oil; heat pan over medium-high heat until just hot. (You can test the readiness of the pan by dropping in a small drop of batter.)

Pour scant ¼ cup of batter in the pan and quickly tilt pan in all directions so that batter covers bottom of pan in a thin film.

Cook crêpe for about 1 minute, or until top of crêpe is no longer liquid. Lift edge of crêpe to test for doneness. The crêpe is ready for flipping when it can be easily shaken loose from the bottom of the pan. Flip the crêpe and cook for about ½ minute on the other side.

Crêpes can be frozen. To reheat, place them in a covered, oven-proof dish in a 300° F oven until thawed.

Note: This recipe is just right for those mornings when family members can't agree on the same thing. The batter can be used to prepare both crêpes and waffles. You can easily prepare both; while the waffles are cooking in the waffle iron, you can make the crêpes.

Serves 3-4 (about 10 crêpes or waffles)

Yogurt Blender Pancakes

2 eggs
2 cups (δ oz.) plain yogurt
4 tbsp vegetable oil
2 cups unsifted all-purpose flour
2 tbsp sugar
2 tsp baking powder
I tsp baking soda
I tsp salt

Blueberry Cinnamon Topping
2 cups blueberry yogurt
4 tbsp honey
½ tsp ground cinnamon

In blender container, blend eggs, yogurt and oil until smooth. Add all dry ingredients; blend until smooth.

On lightly greased hot griddle, pour scant ¼ cup batter for each pancake. When top of pancake is covered with bubbles, turn over. Cook second side I to 2 minutes.

Serve with butter and syrup or Blueberry Cinnamon Topping.

Blueberry Cinnamon Topping: In small saucepan, combine ingredients. Cook over low heat until warm; do not boil. Serve over pancakes.

Serves 4

Crispy Waffles

1 ¾ cups whipping cream
1 ½ cups all-purpose flour, sifted
1 cup cold water
¼ cup melted butter

In a small bowl, whip the cream until fluffy.

In a large bowl, beat together flour, water and a bit of the whipped cream.

Fold in the rest of the whipped cream and the melted butter. Place in refrigerator and let chill for 1 hour.

Heat waffle iron and brush lightly with butter. Pour in batter and cook until done.

Serve with additional whipped cream as a topping, if desired.

Serves 3-4

Southern Waffles

1 cup boiling water
1 cup yellow cornmeal
2 cups all-purpose flour, sifted
3 tsp baking powder
1 ¼ tsp salt
1 tbsp sugar
2 cups milk
3 egg yolks, beaten well
3 tbsp melted butter
2 egg whites, beaten stiff

In a large mixing bowl, pour boiling water over cornmeal; set aside.

In another bowl, sift flour once and measure; add baking powder, salt and sugar and sift again.

Add milk to cornmeal; stir in egg yolks and flour, mixing well.

Stir in melted butter and gently fold in egg whites.
Cook on hot waffle iron.
Serve warm with syrup, if desired.

Serves 4 (approx. 12 waffles)

Sift 2 cups of flour into mixing bowl.

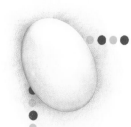

BETTER CHEDDAR OMELET

4 eggs, separated
3 tbsp water
½ cup mayonnaise
½ cup chopped mushrooms (optional)

½ cup diced cooked ham
2 tbsp butter
1 cup shredded Cheddar cheese
Salt and pepper to taste

Preheat oven to 350° F.

In a large bowl, beat egg whites only until soft peaks form.

In a separate bowl, beat together egg yolks, water and mayonnaise. Gently fold yolk mixture into whites. Add mushrooms and ham. Season with salt and pepper. In an oven-proof skillet, melt butter and pour in egg mixture.

Cook over low heat without stirring for 10 minutes, or until egg mixture has become lightly browned on bottom but still remains moist on top.

Transfer skillet to oven and bake for 5 minutes. Sprinkle cheese on top and bake 1 to 2 minutes more, or until cheese melts.

Remove from oven. Loosen edges from side of pan and make a shallow cut through the center so that omelet will fold more easily.

Fold omelet in half and serve.

Serves 2

Spanish Omelet

2 tsp olive oil
1 small onion, minced
1 small potato, sliced
1 tomato, seeded and diced
1 tbsp minced fresh parsley
4 eggs, beaten
Salt to taste

In a large non-stick frying pan over medium heat, add 1 tsp olive oil; fry the onion and the potato in the olive oil until the potatoes are tender.

Add the tomato and parsley and cook until most of liquid has evaporated from the tomatoes.

Transfer mixture to a large bowl and stir in eggs and salt.

Wipe out the frying pan then place it over medium-high heat and let stand for about 2 minutes.

Add 1 tsp olive oil and swirl the pan to coat it. Add the egg mixture; lift and rotate pan so that the eggs are evenly distributed. Turn the heat to low, cover the pan and cook eggs until the top is set. Invert onto a serving plate.
Cut into wedges and serve.

Serves 4

Puffy Omelet

4 egg whites
4 egg yolks
3 oz. sliced bacon, cut into thin strips
¼ cup shredded Cheddar cheese
½ tsp chopped fresh basil
¼ tsp white pepper
5 tsp butter or margarine
½ cup chopped fresh mushrooms
¼ cup chopped green pepper
1 large tomato, peeled, seeded and chopped

In a large bowl, beat egg whites until stiff peaks form.
In a separate bowl, beat egg yolks until thick and lemon-colored; stir in bacon, cheese, half of the basil, and pepper. Fold yolk mixture into egg whites.

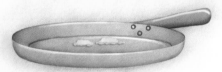

In a 10-inch skillet with oven-proof handle, heat 2 tsp of the butter over medium heat. Spoon egg mixture into skillet, gently smoothing the surface. Reduce heat to low; cook for 7 to 8 minutes or until bottom is golden. Bake in a 350° F. oven for 10-12 minutes.

Meanwhile, in a separate skillet, cook mushrooms and green pepper in the remaining hot butter over medium heat for 3 minutes, or until tender. Add the remaining basil and tomato; cook 5 minutes or until liquid is reduced, stirring occasionally.

Loosen sides of omelet with spatula. Make a shallow cut across omelet, cutting slightly off-center. Spoon filling over larger half, tip skillet and fold the smaller portion of omelet over larger half. Slip omelet onto a warm serving platter. Serve immediately.

Serves 2

RED, YELLOW & WHITE OMELET

1 tsp butter or margarine
1 sweet red pepper, thinly sliced
1 sweet yellow pepper, thinly sliced
4 egg whites
1 tsp chopped fresh basil or ½ tsp dried basil
¼ tsp black pepper
2 tsp grated Parmesan cheese

In a large non-stick frying pan over medium heat, add butter; cook the red pepper and yellow pepper for 4 to 5 minutes, stirring frequently. Keep warm over low heat.

In a small bowl, lightly whisk together the egg whites, basil and black pepper. Grease a small non-stick frying pan with butter or margarine; warm over medium-high heat.

Add half of the egg mixture and swirl the pan to evenly coat the bottom; cook until the eggs are set. Carefully loosen and flip; cook until firm. Sprinkle half of the peppers over the eggs, fold to enclose the filling.

Transfer to a plate and sprinkle with 1 tsp of the Parmesan cheese. Repeat with the remaining egg mixture, peppers and 1 tsp cheese.

Serves 2

Oven French Toast

2 tsp sugar
¼ tsp salt
2 eggs
1 cup milk
¼ cup salad oil
8 slices bread

Preheat oven to 450° F.

In a shallow dish, mix together the sugar, salt and eggs; stir until well blended.

Stir in milk and oil.

Dip both sides of bread slices into mixture and place on well-greased pan.

Bake in oven for about 10 minutes, or until nicely browned.

Serves 4-8

ORANGE POWER SHAKE

½ cup fortified soy milk (plain or vanilla-flavored)
½ cup orange juice
1 tbsp skim milk powder (optional – for extra protein)
¼ cup plain or vanilla-flavored yogurt
(optional – for extra protein and thickness)

Place all desired ingredients in blender; process until smooth and frothy.

Pour into your favorite cup and enjoy!

Serves 1

Granola Crunch

2 cups oatmeal
½ cup chopped almonds
½ cup wheat germ
¼ cup honey
¼ cup vegetable oil
1 tsp vanilla extract
½ cup dried cranberries
½ cup milk, soy milk, or rice milk (optional)

Preheat oven to 325° F.

In a large bowl, use a spoon to mix together the oatmeal, almonds and wheat germ.

In a small bowl, blend together the honey, oil, and vanilla.

Work the honey, oil and vanilla mixture into the oat mixture. Use your (clean) hands to make sure it's well mixed.

Spread the mixture onto a non-stick baking sheet.

Bake for 15 minutes and then remove the baking sheet from the oven.

Use a mixing spoon to stir the mixture around a little on the baking sheet, and then add the dried cranberries.

Return baking sheet back to oven; bake for 10 minutes more.

Remove granola from oven and allow to cool.

For breakfast, serve ½ cup granola with ½ cup milk in a cereal bowl.

Also makes a great snack.

Serves 8

Note: You can prepare granola before hand and store it in an airtight container to preserve freshness and crunch.

Breakfast Bran Muffins

3 tbsp butter, at room temperature
¼ cup molasses
1 egg
1 cup bran cereal
¾ cup buttermilk
1 cup sifted all-purpose flour
1 tsp baking powder
½ tsp baking soda
½ tsp salt
½ cup raisins

Preheat oven to 400° F.

In a large mixing bowl, beat together the butter and molasses.
Add egg and beat well. Add bran cereal and buttermilk;
let stand for 5 minutes.

In a separate bowl, sift together flour, baking powder,
soda and salt.

Add wet mixture to flour mixture and stir
until just moistened. Stir in raisins.

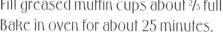

Fill greased muffin cups about ⅔ full.
Bake in oven for about 25 minutes.

Makes 9 large muffins

Bananarama Muffins

½ cup butter or margarine
1 cup sugar
1 egg, well beaten
1 cup mashed bananas (about 2 medium)
1 ½ cups all-purpose flour
1 tsp baking soda, dissolved in 3 tbsp water
1 tsp vanilla
Dash of nutmeg
Pinch of salt

Preheat oven to 375° F.

In a large bowl, cream together butter and sugar. Add egg, bananas, flour, dissolved soda, vanilla, nutmeg and salt. Mix well.

Spoon mixture into greased muffin tins (⅔ full), or into paper cup-lined pans.

Bake in oven for 15-20 minutes.

Makes 14-16 muffins

Spoon mixture into greased muffin tins.

Coco-Banana Milk

16 oz. milk
1 peeled banana
1 tbsp shredded coconut
1 tbsp honey

Place all ingredients in a blender and process until smooth.
Pour into tall glasses and serve.

Serves 2

Good M-o-o-rning Cocoa

1 cup sugar
½ cup unsweetened cocoa
Pinch of salt
2 cups boiling water
1 ½ quarts milk, scalded

In a medium saucepan, combine sugar, cocoa and salt; stir well.
Gradually add water, stirring constantly. Bring to a boil; boil 3 minutes. Remove from heat. Stir in hot milk; beat 2 minutes with wire whisk, being careful not to splash hot liquid.

Makes 8 cups

Peach Yogurt Smoothie

2 ½ cups peeled and diced peaches
1 cup milk
8-oz. carton vanilla yogurt

Place all ingredients in an electric blender. Blend until smooth.
Serve in tall glasses.

Serves 2

Orange Breakfast Nog

½ of a 6-oz. can frozen orange juice
    concentrate (thawed)
1 cup vanilla ice cream
1 cup milk
2 eggs
1 tbsp sugar

Place all ingredients in a blender; process at low speed until well-combined.
Then blend at high speed for about 30 seconds until foamy.

Serves 3 or 4

My best friend in the second grade brought a peanut butter and jelly sandwich to school each and every day. The type of bread never changed, nor did the brand of peanut butter or jelly. I, on the other hand, usually bought my lunch in the cafeteria.

Later on, as a mom, coming up with ideas to fill my sons' superhero-adorned lunchboxes proved to be quite a task. On occasion I would go and join my younger son in kindergarten for lunch. As I looked around at the attempts parents had made to send enticing food to school with their little ones, I realized I was not the only one struggling with making lunchbox lunches interesting.

This chapter contains a variety of tasty and creative lunch ideas to help ease your child through the middle of the school day. Allowing them the opportunity to share in the preparation will make the results all the more enjoyable!

Note: The mother of my best friend, who ate the peanut butter and jelly sandwich each and every day, later became head of the school cafeteria!

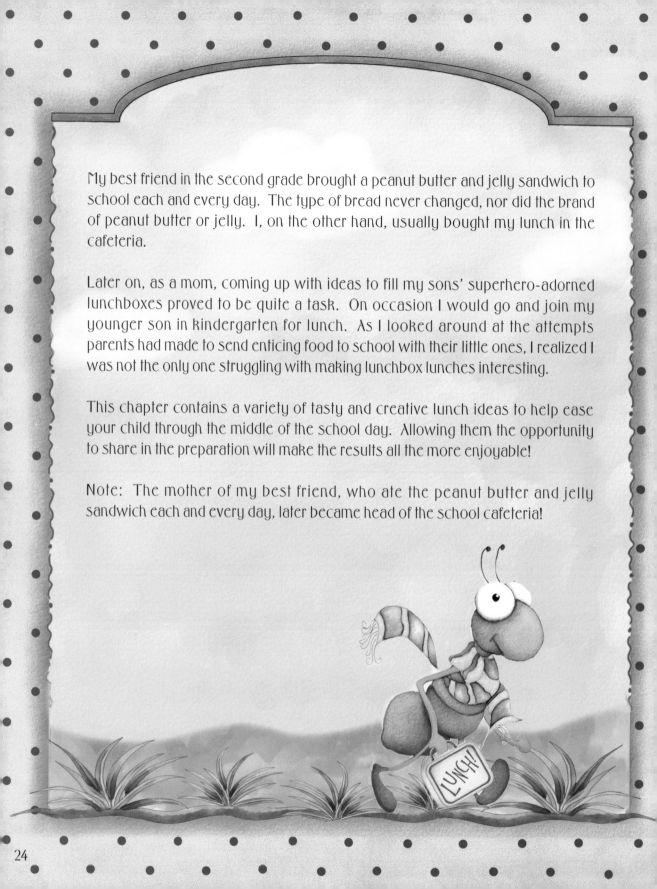

Lunchbox Specials

Chicken Tortilla Roll-Ups

1 cup shredded cooked chicken
⅛ cabbage, shredded
1 medium carrot, grated
½ cup dried apricots, chopped
½ cup mayonnaise
½ tbsp rice vinegar
5 (7-inch) flour tortillas

In a mixing bowl, combine chicken, cabbage, carrot and apricots. Stir in mayonnaise and vinegar; mix well.

Place a spoonful of filling in the center of each tortilla; roll up tightly. Wrap in plastic wrap to hold together. Keep refrigerated.

Serves 5

Roll up filled tortillas tightly and wrap in plastic.

Food Safety Tip:
Add an ice pack to your child's lunchbox.

★ ★ ★ ★ ★

Here's a quick, portable lunch that's low in fat and packed with fiber and essential nutrients. The idea is to pack up the ingredients you need for this meal the night before and, if there is access to a microwave, cook the meal at school.

1 cup cooked brown rice
¾ cup canned kidney beans, rinsed and drained
½ cup frozen corn
½ to ¾ cup canned, diced tomatoes
¼ cup diced green pepper
2 tbsp finely chopped onion
¼ to ½ tsp chili powder

In a microwave-safe plastic container combine rice, beans, corn, tomatoes, green pepper, onion and chili powder. Place lid on container and shake gently, until mixed together.

Place in refrigerator overnight. At school: microwave on HIGH, loosely covered, for 2 to 3 minutes or until hot. Stir before serving.

Serves 2-3

Macaroni-Chicken Salad

2 cups uncooked seashell macaroni
2 cups sliced celery
2 cups chopped cooked chicken
2 large tomatoes, diced
½ cup finely chopped bell pepper
2 tbsp minced onion
1 cup mayonnaise
2 tsp mustard
Salt and pepper to taste

Cook the shell macaroni according to package directions; rinse and drain.

In a large bowl, stir together the macaroni, celery, chicken, tomatoes, pepper and onion.

In a small bowl, mix together the mayonnaise and mustard.

Add the dressing to the macaroni salad and toss to coat. Season to taste with salt and pepper.

Cover and chill in the fridge for 3-4 hours.

Serves 6

Food Safety Tip:

Add an ice pack to your child's lunchbox.

Tuna Pizza Toast

3-oz. can tuna, drained
¼ cup Ketchup
¼ tsp dried oregano
⅛ tsp garlic powder
4 bread slices
¼ cup shredded cheese

In a small bowl, mix together the tuna, Ketchup, oregano and garlic powder.
Toast bread; spread with tuna mixture.
Sprinkle cheese on top.
Place in baking pan and broil in oven until cheese is melted.

Serves 2

Hamwiches

⅓ cup deviled ham
1 cup cottage cheese
1 tbsp minced onion
2 tbsp sweet pickle relish
3 tbsp sour cream
8 bread slices

In a medium bowl, combine ham, cottage cheese, onion, pickle relish and sour cream; mix well. (Mixture can be prepared the evening before and refrigerated.)
When ready to use, spread mixture on 4 bread slices.
Cover with remaining bread slices.

Makes 4 sandwiches

Make your own lunch by spreading ham mixture on your choice of bread.

Cheesy Egg Sandwich

3 hard-cooked eggs
½ cup mayonnaise or salad dressing
1 cup (4 oz.) shredded Cheddar cheese
¼ cup finely chopped celery
8 slices sandwich bread
4 tomato slices (optional)
4 lettuce leaves (optional)

In a bowl, chop the hard-boiled eggs very fine. Stir in mayonnaise, shredded cheese and celery. Chill thoroughly.

For each sandwich, spread ½ cup chilled egg mixture onto 1 slice of bread. Add 1 tomato slice and 1 lettuce leaf, if desired.

Top with another slice of bread and press together lightly.

Makes 4 sandwiches

Food Safety Tip:

Add an ice pack to your child's lunchbox.

Bacon, Ham and Leek Quiche

6 strips bacon
½ cup diced ham
12 leeks, thinly sliced
1 ½ cups shredded Swiss
    cheese
1 tbsp all-purpose flour
1 cup egg substitute
1 cup light cream
1 cup milk
9-inch prepared pie shell

Preheat oven to 375° F.

Fry bacon until crisp. Drain, reserving 1 tbsp of drippings.

Fry ham and leeks in bacon drippings until leeks are tender (5-10 minutes); drain.

In a bowl, mix Swiss cheese with flour; set aside.

In a separate bowl, mix together egg substitute, cream, and milk. Add cheese and flour mixture and mix well. Stir in crumbled bacon, ham and leeks. Mix well to combine. Pour mixture into 9-inch pie shell.

Bake about 45 minutes, or until knife inserted in center comes out clean.

Cut into wedges to serve.

Serves 8

A to Z
Lunchbox Pancakes

¾ cup plain yogurt
1 cup milk
2 eggs, beaten
¼ cup melted butter
1 ½ cups whole wheat flour
¾ tsp baking powder
¾ tsp baking soda
¾ tsp salt
½ cup fruit (fresh, puréed, or canned)

In a small bowl, combine yogurt, milk, eggs and butter, stirring well.

In a large bowl, stir together dry ingredients.

Add yogurt mixture, stirring until batter is smooth and thick.

Fill an empty (clean) ketchup or mustard bottle with batter. Cut off the nozzle to enlarge the opening.

Heat greased non-stick frying pan over medium heat.

To make pancakes, squeeze batter from bottle into frying pan, making alphabet letters.

If batter is too thick, add small amount of milk to squeeze bottle and shake well.

Cook for 2 minutes, or until bubbles appear on the surface, then turn and cook other side for 1-2 minutes, or until browned.

Cool in refrigerator and freeze in freezer-safe container.

Serve 2-3 (frozen) alphabet pancakes in your child's lunchbox with ½ cup of fresh berries, puréed fruit, applesauce, or canned fruit. Pancakes should thaw by lunchtime.

Makes 10-12

Classic Chicken Sandwich

1 cup diced cooked chicken
½ cup chopped celery
¼ cup mayonnaise
½ tsp salt
Pepper to taste

In a bowl, combine chicken with all remaining ingredients; mix gently.
Spread mixture on bread slices.

Makes 4 sandwiches

Where's Waldo Sandwich

1 whole wheat Kaiser roll, cut in half
¼ cup home-made (or deli-made) chicken salad
3 very thin apple slices
2 thin slices Cheddar cheese

Layer bottom half of each roll with ¼ cup chicken salad, apple slices and Cheddar cheese.

Top with tops of rolls.

Serves 1

Food Safety Tip:

Add an ice pack to your child's lunchbox.

Quick Lunchbox Rollers

1 whole wheat tortilla
½ tbsp honey mustard
½ tbsp mayonnaise
2 slices deli ham, turkey, roast beef,
or chicken
½ cup shredded mozzarella cheese
¼ cup shredded lettuce
¼ cup shredded carrots

Lay tortilla flat.
Spread on mustard and mayonnaise.
Arrange deli meat, cheese, lettuce and carrots in center of tortilla.
Roll up tortilla and wrap tightly in plastic wrap to hold together in lunchbox.

Makes 1

Little Helper

Spread tortillas with
mustard and mayo.

Cold Pasta Kebabs

3.5 oz. fresh spinach tortellini
12 cherry tomatoes
½ red bell pepper, cut into 1-inch cubes
½ green bell pepper, cut into 1-inch cubes
6 pitted, jumbo black or green olives (optional)
⅛ cup Italian salad dressing
2 oz. partly skimmed mozzarella cheese, cut into ½-inch cubes
2 oz. cooked turkey sausage, cut into ½-inch slices
6 (10-inch) wooden skewers

In a medium saucepan, cook tortellini in boiling water, according to package directions. Drain and rinse with cold water to stop cooking.

Place tortellini, tomatoes, peppers, (and olives) in a shallow glass dish. Drizzle with Italian salad dressing and allow to sit at room temperature for 30 minutes.

Add mozzarella and turkey sausage. Gently toss to coat with dressing.

Alternating, thread tortellini, tomatoes, green pepper, cheese cubes, red pepper, and turkey sausage on skewers. Top each skewer with an olive. Break off sharp end of skewers. Keep refrigerated.

Makes 6 skewers

CAUTION:
Sharp skewers may be dangerous. Do not serve to children under 7 years of age.

Food Safety Tip:
Add an ice pack to your child's lunchbox.

Banana Boat

1 whole wheat hot dog bun
2 tbsp natural peanut butter
½ banana (sliced lengthwise) or small
   whole banana

Spread peanut butter on both sides of open
hot dog bun.

Place banana inside bun and close.

To reduce browning of banana, wrap in plastic wrap, and do not refrigerate.

Makes 1

Fruit 'n Nut Crunch Sandwich

Great as an afternoon snack or packed in a lunchbox.

2 crispbread crackers
(RyVita Fruit Crunch or any other crispbread)
1 tbsp cashew butter
2 strawberries, sliced

Spread cashew butter on smooth side of both crispbreads.
Place sliced strawberries on one of the crispbreads.
Make sandwich by placing second crispbread on top of strawberries.

Serves 1

Rainbow Veggies with Creamy Hummus Dip

12 baby carrots
½ cucumber, sliced
½ red bell pepper, sliced
½ yellow bell pepper, sliced
¼ cauliflower

Rinse all vegetables well.
Slice cucumber, red and yellow bell peppers.
Break cauliflower into bite-size florets.
Place cut veggies in a reusable plastic container.
Refrigerate until ready to serve.

Creamy Hummus Dip

I cup plain hummus
½ cup creamed cottage cheese
½ cup plain yogurt
¼ tsp salt
¼ tsp pepper
2 tbsp chopped green onion or chives
(optional)

Little Helper

Rinse vegetables
very well.

In a blender, combine hummus, cottage cheese and yogurt; process until smooth.
Transfer mixture to a large bowl. Stir in salt, pepper and optional onion or chives.
Cover and refrigerate for 2 hours, or until chilled. Serve ½ cup of dip with I cup of cut
vegetables.

Serves 4

Hummus

2 cups canned chickpeas, drained and rinsed
3 cloves garlic, minced
3 tbsp lemon juice
¼ cup water
4 tbsp toasted sesame seeds
1 tbsp sesame oil
1 tsp salt

Place the chickpeas, garlic, lemon juice and water in a food processor or blender.
Process until smooth, stopping two or three times to scrape down sides of bowl.
Add the remaining ingredients and process until smooth. If too thick, add more water.
Spread the dip into a shallow bowl. Chill until ready to serve.
Serve with wedges of warm pita bread and/or fresh cup-up vegetables.

Serves 10

Food Safety Tip:

Add an ice pack
to your child's
lunchbox.

Mini Muffin-Wiches

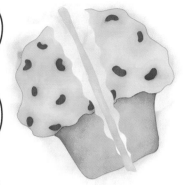

1 mini apple-nut muffin (store bought or home-made)
1 thick slice Cheddar cheese

To make muffin-wich, cut mini muffin in half, from the top down.
Place slice of Cheddar cheese in center of muffin.

Other mini muffin-wich suggestions:
Mini cranberry muffin and chicken breast slices
Mini banana bran muffin and apple butter
Mini cornmeal muffin and tuna salad

Food Safety Tip:
Add an ice pack to your child's lunchbox.

Serves 1

Sweet and Crunchy Snack Mix

½ cup unsweetened crunchy cereal
¼ cup unsalted peanuts or other nuts
¼ cup sunflower seeds
¼ cup raisins or other dried fruit
¼ cup dried banana slices
¼ cup dried apple slices
¼ cup mini chocolate chips (optional)

Mix all ingredients together in a reusable plastic container; shake well.
Portion out ¼ cup of snack mix into snack-size plastic bags.

Makes 7 (¼ cup) servings

Veggie Deviled Eggs

6 hard-cooked eggs, peeled and cut lengthwise
3 to 4 tbsp light mayonnaise or salad dressing
1 tbsp finely chopped sweet red pepper
1 tbsp finely chopped green onion
1 tbsp finely chopped celery
1 tsp yellow mustard
¼ tsp ground black pepper
¼ tsp salt
Paprika for garnish

Cut eggs in half lengthwise. Remove yolks and place in a small bowl.

With fork, mash yolks; add mayonnaise, red pepper, onion, celery, mustard, salt and pepper; mix thoroughly to combine.

Fill the empty egg white shells with the mixture and sprinkle lightly with paprika.
Serve immediately or store covered in refrigerator. Use within 3 days.

Serves 6

Roast Beef and Cheese Wraps

2 pkg. (6 oz. each) vegetable-flavored cream cheese
4 (10-inch) flour tortillas
1 cup shredded carrots
1 cup shredded Cheddar cheese
8 lettuce leaves
1 lb. thinly sliced roast beef

Spread cream cheese evenly on one side of each tortilla.
Layer with equal amounts of shredded carrots and Cheddar cheese.
Top each with 2 lettuce leaves and roast beef slices, leaving a ½-inch border around edge.
Roll up tightly and wrap in plastic wrap.

Serves 4

Spread cream cheese evenly on each tortilla.

Easy Yogurt Parfait

¼ cup plain, fat-free yogurt
¼ cup sweetened fruit-flavored yogurt
2 tbsp bran cereal (sticks, buds or flakes)
¼ cup fresh blueberries or sliced strawberries (or any other fresh fruit)

1-cup plastic container with lid
1 snack-size sealable plastic bag
½-cup plastic container with lid
1 plastic spoon

Combine plain and fruit yogurts
together in a 1-cup plastic container. Cover with a leak-proof lid and refrigerate.

Pour bran cereal in a snack-size sealable plastic bag; close bag.
Place fruit in a ½-cup plastic container. Cover with a leak-proof lid and refrigerate.

Food Safety Tip:

Add an ice pack
to your child's
lunchbox.

At school: add bran cereal and fruit to yogurt; stir and enjoy.

Serves 1

Chewy Cereal Bars

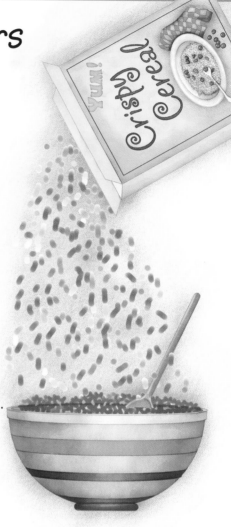

1 ½ cups corn syrup
1 cup brown sugar
½ cup sugar
1 ½ cups peanut butter
6 cups crispy cereal of your choice
¼ cup dried fruit (raisins, cranberries,
cherries, or apricots)

In large microwave-safe bowl, combine corn syrup, brown sugar and sugar and mix well.

Microwave on HIGH for 4-7 minutes until bubbling, stirring twice during cooking cycle.

Remove from microwave and add peanut butter. Stir until peanut butter melts and mixture is smooth.

Add cereal and stir gently but thoroughly until cereal is coated.

Stir in dried fruit.

Spread mixture into a greased 13x9-inch pan. Using back of spoon, press mixture evenly into pan. Let cool and cut into bars.

Makes 24 bars

Banana Nut Bars

¾ cup brown sugar
½ cup butter, softened
1 cup orange marmalade
1 tsp vanilla
2 eggs
2 cups whole wheat flour
¾ cup mashed bananas (about 2 whole bananas)
½ cup chopped walnuts
1 tsp baking powder
½ tsp baking soda
¼ tsp salt
⅓ cup sugar
½ tsp cinnamon

Preheat oven to 350° F. Grease and flour a 15x10-inch baking pan.

In large bowl, combine brown sugar and butter; cream together until well blended.

Add marmalade, vanilla and eggs and blend well.

Add all remaining ingredients, except sugar and cinnamon, and mix until blended thoroughly.

In a small bowl, mix together sugar and cinnamon.

Spread batter into prepared pan and sprinkle with cinnamon sugar.

Bake for 25-30 minutes, or until golden brown.

Cool and cut into bars.

Makes about 30 bars

Little Helper

Sprinkle cinnamon sugar over batter in pan.

A busy school day can really whet a child's appetite. When my sons would burst in the front door at the end of their school day, they would immediately head for the kitchen. You'd think they hadn't eaten in days! And heaven help you if the cupboards were short on munchies when they were on the hunt for sustenance.

At first, I found it somewhat of a challenge to make sure the kitchen was stocked with "good" food to divert the kids from heading for the candy and chips. Satisfying their cravings became much easier when I discovered how an easy-to-prepare yummy fruit muffin and creamy smoothie could conveniently do the trick.

Following are several tasty and satisfying snack ideas to rescue you from the after school raid on your kitchen. Enjoy sharing them with your kids.

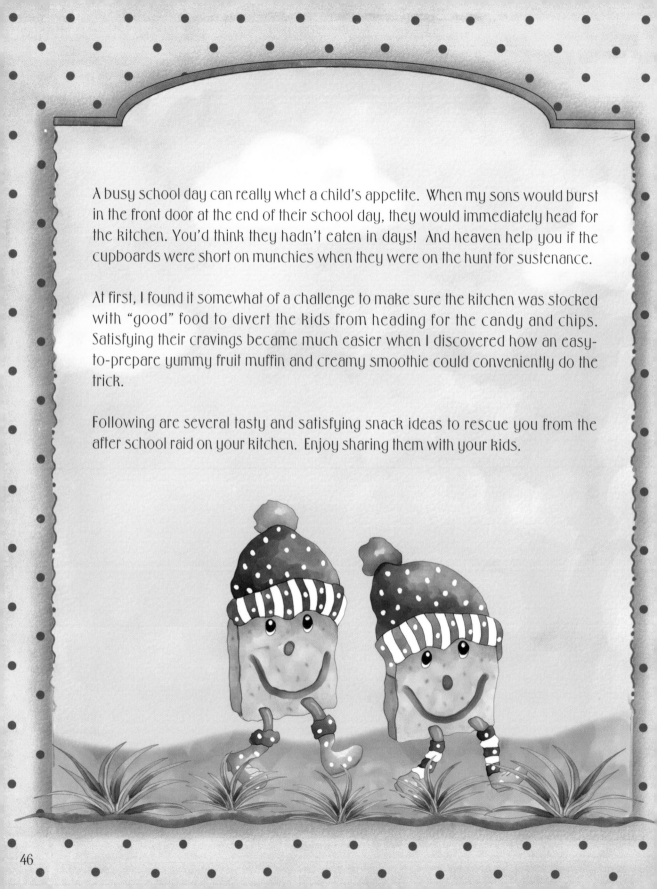

Afternoon Snacks

English Muffin Pizza

1 whole wheat English muffin
4 tbsp pizza sauce
4 tbsp shredded part-skim
mozzarella cheese
2 tbsp diced tomato
2 tbsp diced cooked ham
1 tbsp pineapple pieces

Preheat oven, or toaster oven, to Grill or Broil setting.
Slice English muffin in half. Place the two halves on a small baking sheet.
Spread pizza sauce evenly on muffin halves.
Sprinkle cheese on top of sauce.
Sprinkle tomatoes, ham and pineapple on top of cheese.
Broil until cheese is browned and sauce is bubbly.
Serve immediately.

Serves 1-2

Little Helper

Spread pizza sauce
on muffin halves and
sprinkle with cheese.

After School Special

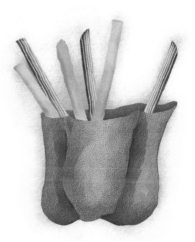

1 extra large green, yellow or red pepper, washed
1 celery stick
1 carrot, washed and peeled
4 tbsp your favorite salad dressing

Cut the pepper in half horizontally. Clean out the seeds from the inside. Cut carrot into skinny sticks, about 2 inches long.
Cut celery into skinny sticks, about 2 inches long. Spoon 2 tbsp of salad dressing in the bottom of each pepper "bowl". Put celery sticks and carrot sticks into each pepper bowl.
Now you've got a portable veggie snack. You can pull out the veggies and eat them with a little dressing. Then when you're finished with the veggies, it's time to eat the bowl!

Serves 2

Cheese Delight

1 lb. shredded Monterey Jack cheese
  with jalapeño peppers
1 lb. shredded Cheddar cheese
1 large can evaporated milk
½ cup all-purpose flour
2 eggs

Preheat oven to 350° F.
Spread cheeses into a 13x9-inch baking dish.
In a small bowl, mix together evaporated milk, flour and eggs.
Pour mixture over cheese.
Bake in oven for 40 minutes.
Cut into squares to serve.

Makes 20-24 pieces

Mexican Ant-eat-o's!

1 flour tortilla (8 or 10 inches in diameter)
¼ cup cream cheese (plain or salsa-flavored)
¼ cup prepared salsa
¼ cup sour cream

Turn oven to Grill or Broil setting while you prepare the tortilla.

Lay tortilla flat. Using a butter knife or back of tablespoon, spread cream cheese evenly in the center of tortilla, leaving a 1-inch border around sides of tortilla. Using a butter knife or back of tablespoon, spread salsa evenly on top of cream cheese.

Roll up tortilla tightly from one end to the other. Cut tortilla into 8-10 even pieces. Each piece should look like a pinwheel when laid flat. Lay pinwheels on a non-stick (or lightly greased) baking sheet.

Place in oven and broil for 3-5 minutes. Flip pinwheels over, cooked side down. Broil for another 3-5 minutes, or until lightly browned and crispy.

Let cool for a few minutes.
Dip in sour cream and enjoy!

Makes 8-10 pieces

Peaches 'n Cream

2 heaping tbsp oat bran
½ cup canned sliced peaches, in light syrup
½ cup peach or vanilla-flavored yogurt
¼ tsp cinnamon

Preheat oven to Grill or Broil setting.

Sprinkle oat bran evenly on a non-stick baking pan. Place under oven grill for a few minutes, watching closely so that it does not burn. When oat bran is lightly toasted, remove from oven and let cool.

Layer peach slices in the bottom of a bowl. Next, layer the yogurt on top of the peach slices. Top with oat bran. Sprinkle with cinnamon.

Serve immediately or cover and refrigerate until ready to eat.

Serves 1

Banana Bread

3 cups sugar
1 cup butter
4 eggs
2 cups mashed bananas
2 tsp vanilla
3 ½ cups all-purpose flour
2 cups chopped pecans
2 tsp baking soda dissolved in ½ cup
buttermilk

Preheat oven to 325° F.

In a large bowl, cream together the sugar and butter; add the eggs and beat well.
Add the mashed bananas and vanilla.
Add the flour, nuts and buttermilk with baking soda dissolved in it.

Pour into 3 greased loaf pans and bake at 325° F for 1 ½ hours.

Makes 3 loaves

CHILI POPCORN

3 cups air-popped popcorn
Butter-flavored cooking spray
1 tsp chili powder seasoning
¼ tsp cayenne pepper
   (optional – caution: it's hot!)

Preheat oven to 300° F.
Put popcorn in a large mixing bowl.
Lightly coat popcorn with butter-flavored cooking spray. Toss and coat again.
Combine chili powder and cayenne pepper.
Sprinkle spices over popcorn and toss to coat evenly.
Spread popcorn evenly in large baking pan.
Bake for 10 minutes, tossing once.

Makes 3 cups

ANTS ON SNOWBOARDS

1 celery stick
3 tbsp fruit-flavored cream cheese
   (eg. pineapple, strawberry)
1 tbsp raisins

Wash the celery and cut it into 3 equal pieces.
Spread cream cheese in u-shaped part of celery, from one end to the other.
Press about 8 raisins gently into cream cheese.

ENJOY!

Serves 1

Granny's Pecan Bars

1 ¼ cups unsifted all-purpose flour
1 cup confectioners´ sugar
⅓ cup unsweetened cocoa
1 cup cold margarine or butter
14-oz. can Eagle Brand Sweetened
Condensed Milk (NOT evaporated milk)
1 egg
2 tsp vanilla extract
1 cup chopped pecans

Preheat oven to 350° F. (325° F. for glass dish.)
In large bowl, combine flour, sugar and cocoa; cut in margarine until crumbly.
Press mixture firmly into bottom of 13x9-inch baking pan. Bake 15 minutes.
In a medium bowl, combine sweetened condensed milk, egg and vanilla; mix well.
Stir in pecans.
Spread mixture evenly over baked crust.
Bake 25 minutes, or until lightly browned.
Cool and cut into bars.
Store covered in refrigerator.

Makes 24-36 bars

Spread pecan
mixture over crust.

Frosted Raisin Bars

1 cup raisins
1 cup water
½ cup vegetable oil
1 egg
1 cup sugar
1 ¾ cups all-purpose flour
1 tsp allspice
½ tsp salt
1 tsp baking soda
1 tsp cinnamon
¼ tsp ground cloves
½ cup chopped nuts

Preheat oven to 350° F.

In a saucepan, boil the raisins in 1 cup of water. Drain and let cool.

In a large bowl, mix together the vegetable oil, egg and sugar.

In a separate bowl, sift together the flour, allspice, salt, baking soda, cinnamon and cloves.

Combine with sugar mixture. Add raisins and nuts.

Spread mixture in a sheet cake pan and bake in oven for 20-25 minutes.

Frost with glazed icing:

1 cup powdered sugar
1 tbsp butter
½ tsp vanilla
2 tbsp milk

In a small bowl, mix together all ingredients until smooth. Spread on hot cake and cut into squares.

Makes 20-24 bars

Berry Crumb Bars

1 cup white sugar
3 cups all-purpose flour
1 tsp baking powder
1 pinch salt
1 pinch ground cinnamon
1 cup shortening
1 egg
4 cups raspberries or other berries
½ cup white sugar
3 tsp cornstarch

Preheat oven to 375° F. Grease a 13x9-inch pan.

In a large bowl, combine 1 cup sugar, flour, baking powder, salt, ground cinnamon, shortening and egg. Dough will be crumbly.

Spread half of the dough into the prepared pan.

In a mixing bowl, combine the berries, ½ cup sugar and cornstarch. Spoon mixture over dough in pan.

Crumble the remaining dough over the top of the berries.

Bake in oven for 45 minutes, or until the top is slightly brown.

Cut into bars to serve.

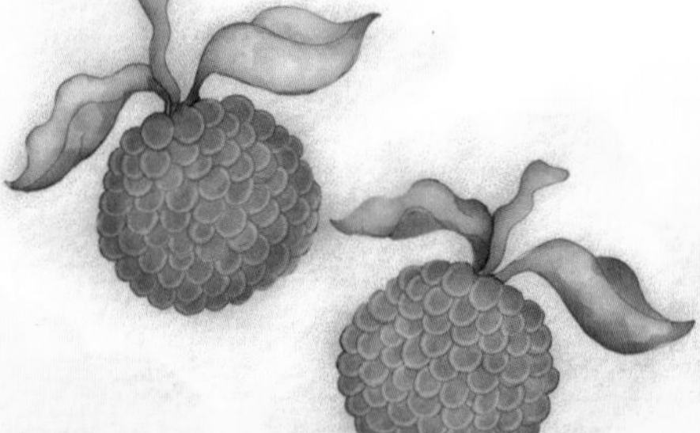

Makes 12-15 bars

Big Batch
Spelt-Bran Blueberry Muffins

5 cups spelt flour
5 ½ cups 100% bran cereal
2 cups packed brown sugar
1 cup frozen blueberries
1 tbsp baking soda
1 tbsp ground cinnamon
4 cups buttermilk
1 cup vegetable oil
4 eggs

Preheat oven to 375° F. Prepare two 12-cup muffin tins, greased or paper-lined.

In a large bowl, combine flour, cereal, brown sugar, blueberries, baking soda and cinnamon.

In another large bowl, mix together buttermilk, oil and eggs. Stir into dry ingredients and mix until moistened.

Spoon batter into muffin cups, filling to ¾ full.

Bake for 25 to 30 minutes, or until golden brown.
Cool in pans for 5 minutes; remove muffins.
Cool muffins on a wire rack before serving.
Store in airtight containers; also freeze, if desired.

Makes 24 muffins

Fruit and Yogurt Muffins

2 cups all-purpose flour
1 cup sugar
1 tsp baking soda
1 tsp baking powder
8-oz. container vanilla yogurt
1 egg
4 tbsp butter, melted
2 cups blueberries or cranberries

Preheat oven to 350° F.
Grease 12 muffin cups or line with paper muffin liners.

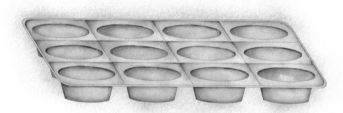

In a large mixing bowl, stir together flour, sugar, baking soda and baking powder.
In a separate bowl, combine yogurt, egg, butter and berries.
Add yogurt mixture into flour, stirring just until combined.
Spoon into prepared muffin cups.
Bake in oven for 25 minutes.

Makes 12 muffins

Apple Oatmeal Cookies

½ cup margarine, softened
½ cup honey
1 egg
1 tsp vanilla extract
¾ cup whole wheat flour
½ tsp baking soda
¾ tsp ground cinnamon
1 ½ cups quick-cooking oats
1 apple, cored and chopped

Preheat the oven to 375° F. Grease cookie sheets.

In a large bowl, cream together the margarine, honey, egg and vanilla until smooth.

In a separate bowl, combine the whole wheat flour, baking soda and cinnamon; stir into the creamed mixture. Mix in oats and apple.

Drop by teaspoonfuls onto prepared cookie sheets.

Bake in oven for 8 to 10 minutes.

Allow cookies to cool on baking sheet for 5 minutes before removing to a wire rack to cool completely.

Makes 4 dozen

Little Helper

Drop cookie dough by spoonfuls onto cookie sheet.

Golden Raisin and Nut Cookies

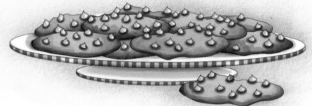

1 cup butter, softened
1 cup light brown sugar
1 cup white sugar
2 eggs
1 tsp vanilla extract
1 ⅛ cups all-purpose flour
1 tsp baking soda

1 tsp baking powder
1 pinch salt
3 cups rolled oats
½ cup wheat germ
1 ¼ cups golden raisins
1 ⅓ cups chopped walnuts

Preheat oven to 350° F. Grease cookie sheets.

In a large bowl, cream together the butter, brown sugar and white sugar until light and fluffy. Add the eggs one at a time, beating well with each addition, then stir in vanilla.

In a separate bowl, combine the flour, baking soda, baking powder, and salt; gradually stir into the creamed mixture.

Finally, stir in the oats, wheat germ, raisins and walnuts.
Drop dough by heaping tablespoonfuls onto prepared cookie sheets.
Wet hands and flatten cookies slightly. (Cookies should be about ¾-inch thick and 2 ½ inches wide before baking.)

Bake 15 to 20 minutes. Allow cookies to cool on baking sheets for 5 minutes before removing to a wire rack to cool completely.

Makes 2 dozen

Cowboy Oatmeal Cookies

2 cups all-purpose flour
½ tsp baking powder
1 tsp baking soda
½ tsp salt
½ cup margarine
½ cup vegetable oil
1 cup packed brown sugar
1 cup white sugar
2 eggs
2 cups quick-cooking oats
1 cup butterscotch chips
½ cup chopped nuts (optional)

Preheat the oven to 350° F.

In a mixing bowl, sift together flour, baking powder, baking soda and salt; set aside.

In a large bowl, cream together margarine, oil, brown sugar and white sugar until smooth. Beat in eggs one at a time. Gradually stir in the sifted ingredients until well blended. Fold in oats, butterscotch chips and nuts.

Drop by spoonfuls onto ungreased cookie sheets.

Bake for 10 to 12 minutes or until lightly brown.

Cool on the cookie sheets for a few minutes before transferring to wire racks to cool completely.

Makes 3 dozen

Fruit-Stacked English Muffin

2 English muffins, split
8-oz. container vanilla yogurt
¾ cup sliced fresh strawberries
¾ cup drained crushed pineapple

Lightly toast English muffin halves in the toaster.
Spread each half with yogurt.
Top each half with strawberries and pineapple.
Serve while English muffins are still warm.

Serves 4

Spread muffin half
with yogurt and top
with fruit.

Fruitti Milkshake

⅔ cup milk
¼ cup sliced strawberries
½ tsp cherry extract
½ tsp orange extract
½ cup sugar
6 ice cubes, crushed

Combine all ingredients, except ice cubes, in blender. Blend at medium speed for 2 minutes, or until strawberries are puréed.
Add crushed ice; blend at medium speed for 2 more minutes.
Serve in a tall glass.

Serves 1

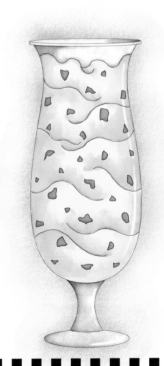

Orange Berry Smoothie

1 ½ cups low-fat vanilla yogurt
3 cups fresh or frozen raspberries (or strawberries)
2 tbsp granulated sugar
1 cup orange (or apple or other flavor) juice

Place yogurt, berries, sugar and juice in blender or food processor; process until smooth. Pour into glasses and serve with cookie on the side.

Serves 4

My childhood neighborhood was home to kids of all ages. After school, once all homework had been completed and all musical instruments practiced, the front yards of our street would begin to fill with kids ready for some energetic play. We would move from yard to yard, chasing each other, playing hide-and-seek, creating neighborhood dramas for our makeshift theatre and doing a myriad of other activities that our vivid imaginations conjured up.

Play would begin to slow down as aromas started wafting out of raised kitchen windows up and down the street. Each kid kept one ear pricked up so as to hear the sound of their mother's first call to supper. We always managed to work up quite an appetite!

One of my favorite suppers was meat loaf. This later became my younger son's favorite evening meal as well. I never had to call him twice on meat loaf night.

Super Suppers

Chicken Delight

6 boneless, skinless chicken breasts
Apricot preserves
1 bottle Russian dressing

Preheat oven to 350° F.

Brush chicken breasts on both sides with apricot preserves.

Place in casserole dish; pour dressing over all.

Bake in oven for 45-50 minutes.

Serves 6

Lemon Chicken

4 chicken breasts
Butter
3 tbsp lemon juice
1 cup water
3 tbsp Worcestershire sauce

In a large skillet, brown chicken breasts in butter.
Add the lemon juice, water and Worcestershire sauce.
Simmer for 1 hour.
Serve with rice.

Serves 4

Chicken Enchilada Casserole

2 ½ cups diced, cooked chicken
1 ½ cups chicken broth
1 can cream of chicken soup
1 can cream of mushroom soup
4-oz. can chopped green chilies, undrained
4-oz. jar chopped pimientos, drained
8-oz. bag tortilla chips, slightly crushed
1 lb. Cheddar cheese, grated

Preheat oven to 350° F.

In a large bowl, mix together all ingredients except tortilla chips and cheese.

Cover the bottom of a greased 13x9-inch baking dish with 1 cup of tortilla chips. Layer in order:

½ chicken mixture
⅓ cheese

Repeat, ending with tortilla chips topped with cheese.

Refrigerate at least 1 hour.

Bake in oven for 45 minutes.

Serves 6-8

Chicken and Rice Bake

1 cut-up frying chicken
1 cup long-grain white rice
1 envelope onion soup mix
1 can cream of chicken soup
1 ½ cans water
4-oz. can sliced mushrooms
1 tsp salt
½ tsp pepper

Preheat oven to 350° F.

Combine all ingredients, except chicken, and spread into a 13x9-inch casserole dish. Arrange the chicken pieces on top.

Cover and bake for 1 hour.

Carefully uncover and stir. Bake an additional 30 minutes, uncovered.

Serves 4-6

Little Helper

Arrange chicken pieces over rice mixture.

Easy Chicken and Dressing Casserole

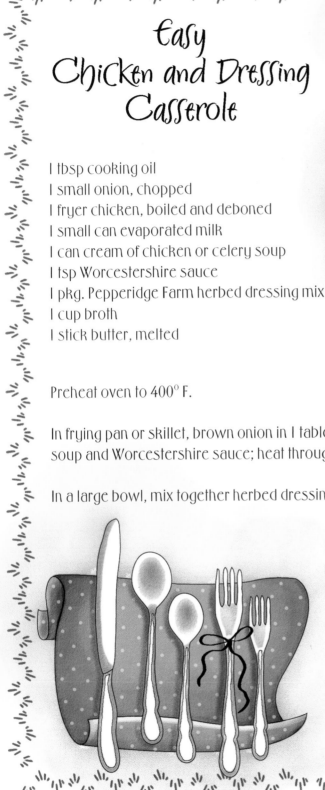

1 tbsp cooking oil
1 small onion, chopped
1 fryer chicken, boiled and deboned
1 small can evaporated milk
1 can cream of chicken or celery soup
1 tsp Worcestershire sauce
1 pkg. Pepperidge Farm herbed dressing mix
1 cup broth
1 stick butter, melted

Preheat oven to 400° F.

In frying pan or skillet, brown onion in 1 tablespoon of oil; add chicken pieces, milk, soup and Worcestershire sauce; heat through.

In a large bowl, mix together herbed dressing, broth and melted butter.

In a casserole dish, layer chicken mixture alternately with dressing mixture. End with dressing on top.

Bake in oven for 20-30 minutes.

Serves 4

My Favorite Meat Loaf

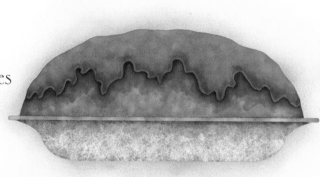

Meat Loaf
1 ½ lbs. ground beef
1 egg
1 slice bread, torn into small pieces
1 tsp garlic powder
4 oz. tomato sauce

Sauce Topping
3 tbsp brown sugar
2 tbsp mustard
2 tbsp Worcestershire sauce
8 oz. tomato sauce

Preheat oven to 350° F.

In a large bowl, mix together all meat loaf ingredients and form into a loaf. Place in a shallow loaf pan or casserole dish.

In a separate bowl, combine all ingredients for sauce topping and spread over meat loaf.

Bake uncovered in oven for 1 ½ hours.

Serves 6

Tear bread slice into small pieces.

70

Shepherd's Pie

8 potatoes, peeled and cubed
1 egg yolk
½ cup cream
2 tbsp butter
1 cup finely chopped onion
1 cup finely chopped celery
2 tbsp olive oil
1 ½ lbs. lean ground beef
1 cup beef broth
1 tsp Worcestershire sauce
¼ tsp garlic powder
Salt and pepper to taste
1 can creamed corn
½ cup shredded Cheddar cheese (optional)

Boil potatoes in water until tender; drain and place in a large bowl.

Combine egg yolk and cream; add the cream to potatoes along with butter. Mash until potatoes are smooth.

While potatoes are boiling, in a large skillet over medium heat, sauté onions and celery in olive oil until tender.

Stir in ground beef; brown and crumble meat for a few minutes.

Add beef broth, Worcestershire sauce, garlic powder, salt and pepper; stir and cook over low heat for 15 to 20 minutes.

Pour meat mixture into a casserole dish, top with the creamed corn, spreading evenly.

Top with layer of mashed potatoes.

Sprinkle with Cheddar cheese and bake in a 350° F. oven for 25 to 35 minutes, or until potato topping is puffy and lightly browned.

Serves 6

Meal In-A-Foil

4 formed hamburger patties
1 large onion, sliced
4 potatoes, quartered
4 carrots, sliced thin
4 tbsp butter
Salt and pepper to taste

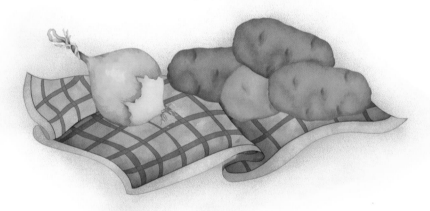

Preheat oven to 375° F.
Tear 4 pieces of foil large enough to enclose patty and vegetables.
Place 1 patty on each piece of foil; add a slice of onion.
Place quartered potato on top of onion slice. Add sliced carrots.
Top each with 1 tbsp of butter. Season with salt and pepper.
Pull foil together; fold at top.
Bake in oven for 1 hour and 30 minutes.
Serve immediately.

Serves 4

Steak Stroganoff

1 lb. round steak, cut in thin stripes
½ cup chopped onion
1 tbsp all-purpose flour
½ tsp salt
¼ tsp garlic powder
1 can condensed cream of mushroom soup
1 cup sour cream
1 pkg. (8 oz.) wide egg noodles

In a large skillet over medium heat, sauté the meat and onions for 10 minutes, or until the meat is browned and the onion is tender.

Stir in the flour, salt and garlic powder. Add the mushroom soup; mix well and cook, uncovered, for 20 minutes.

Reduce heat to low and add the sour cream, stirring well and allowing to heat through.

While the meat mixture cooks, boil the egg noodles according to package directions; drain.

Transfer noodles to serving platter and pour meat mixture on top.

Serve immediately.

Serves 7

Pork and Black Bean Stew

1 ½ lbs. pork, cut in 1-inch cubes
½ cup all-purpose flour
½ tsp salt
¼ tsp ground black pepper
2 tbsp olive oil
1 ½ cups chopped onions
½ lb. pork sausage
1 can condensed chicken broth
3 large cloves garlic, minced
2 tsp chopped fresh parsley
½ tsp dried oregano
1 to 2 cans (15 oz. each) black beans, drained, rinsed
1 cup frozen corn kernels
1 large red bell pepper, diced
2 plum tomatoes, diced
1 tsp lemon juice
Diced tomato and green onion for garnish (optional)

Toss pork cubes in a food storage bag with flour, salt and pepper; shake to coat.
Heat olive oil in a large skillet. Add pork cubes and brown on all sides. Transfer meat to crock pot.
Add onions and pork sausage to skillet and brown lightly; add to crock pot.
Add the chicken broth and garlic. Cook on HIGH for 4 ½ to 6 hours.
About 1 hour before end of cooking time, add parsley, oregano, black beans, corn, bell pepper, plum tomatoes and lemon juice.
Serve with cornbread and a garnish of diced tomatoes and green onions.

Serves 6-8

Apple-Stuffed Pork Chops

1 tbsp chopped onion
¼ cup butter or margarine
3 cups fresh bread crumbs
2 cups chopped apples
¼ cup chopped celery
2 tsp chopped fresh parsley
¼ tsp salt
6 (1 ¼-inch) thick pork chops
Salt and pepper to taste
1 tbsp vegetable oil

Preheat oven to 350° F.

In a large skillet, sauté onion in butter until tender; remove from heat. Stir in the bread crumbs, apples, celery, parsley and salt; mix well.

Cut a large pocket on the side of each pork chop; season inside and out with salt and pepper. Spoon apple mixture loosely into pockets.

In a large skillet, heat oil to medium-high and brown chops on both sides. Place browned chops in an ungreased 9x13-inch baking dish.

Cover with aluminum foil and bake in oven for 30 minutes. Remove foil cover and bake for 30 minutes longer, or until juices run clear.

Serves 6

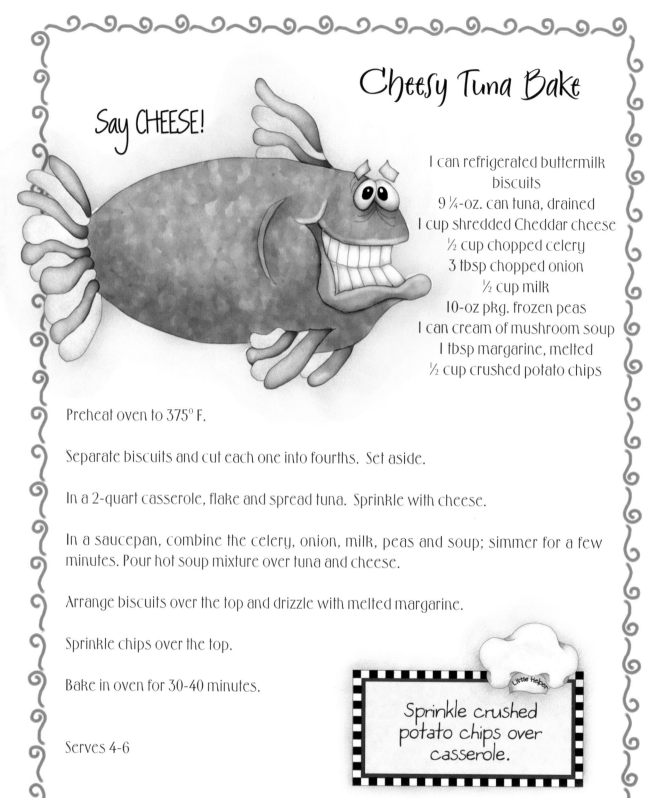

Cheesy Tuna Bake

Say CHEESE!

1 can refrigerated buttermilk biscuits
9 ¼-oz. can tuna, drained
1 cup shredded Cheddar cheese
½ cup chopped celery
3 tbsp chopped onion
½ cup milk
10-oz pkg. frozen peas
1 can cream of mushroom soup
1 tbsp margarine, melted
½ cup crushed potato chips

Preheat oven to 375° F.

Separate biscuits and cut each one into fourths. Set aside.

In a 2-quart casserole, flake and spread tuna. Sprinkle with cheese.

In a saucepan, combine the celery, onion, milk, peas and soup; simmer for a few minutes. Pour hot soup mixture over tuna and cheese.

Arrange biscuits over the top and drizzle with melted margarine.

Sprinkle chips over the top.

Bake in oven for 30-40 minutes.

Serves 4-6

Little Helper

Sprinkle crushed potato chips over casserole.

Fish 'n Chips

1 lbs. white fish fillets
1 tbsp fresh lemon juice
3 baking potatoes
Ice water
1 ½ cups flour
½ tsp baking powder
½ tsp salt
2 eggs, beaten
1 cup beer
Oil for deep-frying

Cut fish into medium-size pieces (2 pieces per serving); sprinkle with lemon juice.

Peel potatoes and cut into slices; then into strips. Place potato strips in bowl of ice water for 5 minutes; drain and dry on paper towels.

In a bowl, combine 1 cup flour, baking powder, salt, eggs and beer. Stir until batter is smooth and creamy.

Dredge fish in remaining flour and then dip in batter, making sure each fillet is well coated.

Drop battered fillets in prepared deep fryer and cook until batter is crisp and golden. Drain fish well on paper towels; keep warm in preheated 300° F. oven.

Drop the potatoes slices into fryer and cook until golden brown. Remove, drain on paper towels and serve with fish.

Serves 4-6

Cheesy Spaghetti Casserole

1 ½ lbs. lean ground beef
3 cups tomato sauce
4 ½ cups water
3 pkgs. spaghetti sauce mix
¾ tsp salt
1 ½ lbs. spaghetti
¼ cup butter
⅓ cup all-purpose flour
1 ½ tsp salt
2 cups evaporated milk
1 cup water
2 cups shredded American cheese
⅓ cup grated Parmesan cheese

In a large saucepan, brown meat; drain fat. Add tomato sauce, 4 ½ cups water, sauce mix and ¾ tsp salt. Simmer, uncovered, for 30 minutes, stirring often.
Break spaghetti into thirds. Cook according to package directions; rinse. Drain and keep warm.

Preheat oven to 350° F.

Melt butter in saucepan; stir in flour and 1 ½ tsp salt. Add milk and water slowly, stirring over medium heat, until thickened. Add 1 ½ cups American cheese and the Parmesan cheese. Stir until melted.

Divide each quantity of spaghetti, tomato sauce and cheese sauce in half.

In two 13x9x2-inch casserole dishes, layer ingredients as follows: spaghetti, half of tomato sauce, cheese sauce, spaghetti and remaining tomato sauce. Top with remaining shredded American cheese. Bake in oven for 15-25 minutes, or until bubbly. Serve at once.

Serves 12

Mama's Lasagna

1 box (8 oz.) lasagna noodles
1 tbsp olive oil
4 cloves garlic, minced
1 small onion, diced
1 ½ lbs. ground beef
3 cups canned tomato sauce
Oregano to taste
2 cups ricotta cheese
2 eggs
¼ cup milk
1 cup shredded mozzarella cheese
¾ cup grated Parmesan cheese

Cook noodles according to package instructions; drain and rinse.

Preheat oven to 375° F.

Heat olive oil in skillet and sauté garlic and onions for about 5 minutes. Add the ground beef; brown the meat and drain excess fat.

In a large saucepan, combine meat mixture, tomato sauce and oregano;
simmer 15-20 minutes.

In a medium bowl, mix together ricotta cheese, eggs and milk.

In a 9x13-inch buttered baking pan, layer ⅓ of the lasagna noodles, cover with ⅓ of the meat sauce, then ⅓ of the ricotta cheese mixture, mozzarella cheese, and Parmesan cheeses. Repeat layers twice.

Bake, covered, for 30 minutes; uncover and bake for 1 minute.
Let stand for 8 to 10 minutes before serving.

Serves 8-10

Chili Billy

2 lbs. hamburger meat
1 large onion, chopped
1 clove garlic, chopped or
　1/8 tsp garlic powder
1 1/2 tsp cumin

2 tsp chili powder
3 cups tomato juice
1 cup water
15-oz. can chili beans
Salt to taste

In a large pot, brown meat with onion and garlic.
Add remaining ingredients, except beans, and cook for 1 1/2 hours.
Add the beans and cook an additional 30 minutes.

Serves 4

Hamburger in a Pea Patch

1 lb. ground beef
1 pkg. onion gravy mix
1/4 tsp garlic salt
1 1/2 cups water
1/3 cup rice, uncooked
10-oz. pkg. frozen peas, thawed
1 can French-fried onions
Soy sauce (optional)

In a frying pan or skillet, brown ground beef and drain fat.
Stir in gravy mix, garlic salt, water and uncooked rice. Bring to a boil.
Reduce heat to low, cover and simmer for 15 minutes.
Stir in thawed peas.
Continue simmering until rice is tender.
Stir in onions.
Serve with soy sauce, if desired.

Serves 4-6

Super Macaroni and Cheese

1 cup uncooked elbow macaroni
2 eggs, beaten
1 cup milk
1 cup cottage cheese
1 ¼ cups shredded sharp Cheddar cheese
½ tsp salt
¼ tsp black pepper
Vegetable cooking spray
1 tbsp fine, dry bread crumbs

Preheat oven to 350° F.

In a large pot, cook macaroni according to package directions, omitting salt; drain.

Combine macaroni and the next 6 ingredients.

Spoon mixture into a 1-quart baking dish coated with cooking spray.

Sprinkle bread crumbs over mixture.

Bake in oven for 1 hour.

Serves 6

Little Helper

Sprinkle bread crumbs over mixture in casserole.

Spaghetti with Meat Sauce

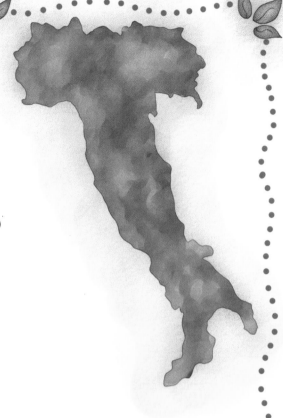

2 tbsp olive oil
½ cup minced onion
2 cloves garlic, minced
½ cup minced celery
2 medium carrots, finely chopped
1 lb. ground beef or pork (or ½ lb. of each)
½ tsp white sugar
1 tsp salt
6 oz. chopped fresh mushrooms
28-oz. can tomatoes
6-oz. can tomato paste
10.5-oz. can beef broth
2 tsp dried basil
1 tsp dried oregano
1 lb. spaghetti
1 tsp olive oil
3 tbsp salt
¼ cup chopped fresh parsley (optional)
Parmesan cheese

Heat oil in a large skillet over medium-low heat; sauté onion, garlic, celery and carrots until onion is transparent.

Add meat and brown for 5 minutes (or until no longer pink), breaking it up with a wooden spoon.

Mix in sugar, salt and mushrooms; lower heat and cook for about 3 minutes.

Add tomatoes, tomato paste, broth, basil and oregano; simmer over low heat for about 2 hours, stirring occasionally.

Meanwhile, cook spaghetti in a large pot of lightly salted boiling water until *al dente*. Drain well.

When ready to serve, spoon meat sauce over cooked pasta, sprinkle Parmesan cheese on top and garnish with parsley.

Serves 6

El Toro Enchiladas

1 lb. lean ground beef
2 medium cans refried beans
1 dozen corn tortillas
1 cup chopped onion
1 large pkg. grated cheese
(eg. Monterey Jack)
2 medium cans chili sauce

Preheat oven to 350° F.

In a skillet, brown the ground beef; drain and set aside.

In a saucepan (or microwave) heat the beans until warm.

Spread the beans on the tortillas. Top with ground beef and onion; sprinkle with cheese.

Fold tortillas and lay in oblong pan. Pour chili sauce over tortillas and top with more cheese.

Bake in oven until cheese melts and enchiladas are brown on top.

Serves 6-8

Beans 'n Franks

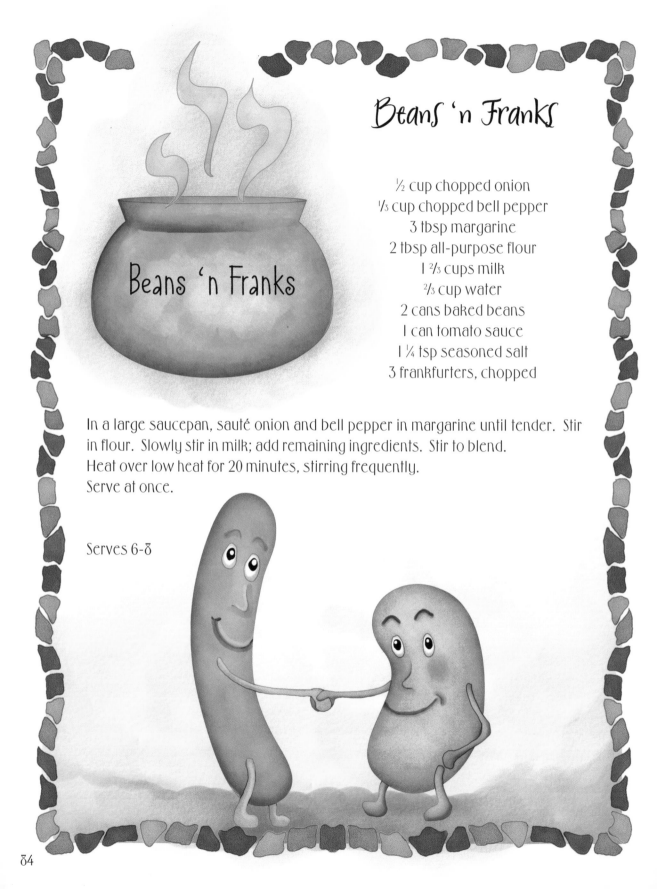

½ cup chopped onion
⅓ cup chopped bell pepper
3 tbsp margarine
2 tbsp all-purpose flour
1 ⅔ cups milk
⅔ cup water
2 cans baked beans
1 can tomato sauce
1 ¼ tsp seasoned salt
3 frankfurters, chopped

In a large saucepan, sauté onion and bell pepper in margarine until tender. Stir in flour. Slowly stir in milk; add remaining ingredients. Stir to blend.
Heat over low heat for 20 minutes, stirring frequently.
Serve at once.

Serves 6-8

Hash-Brown Casserole

½ cup finely chopped onion
¼ cup finely chopped celery
1 ½ tbsp butter
1 can (10 ½ oz.) cream of celery soup
⅓ cup milk
3 oz. cream cheese
4 cups frozen hash brown potatoes
   (loosely packed)
½ cup shredded sharp Cheddar cheese

Preheat oven to 350° F.
In a saucepan, slowly sauté
onion and celery in butter until tender; remove and set aside.
Add soup, milk and cream cheese to saucepan. Cook over medium-low heat, stirring, until smooth.
In a large bowl, combine potatoes with the onions and celery; stir in the soup mixture.
Pour into a 10x7x1½ -inch baking dish. Cover with foil and bake for 1 hour and 15 minutes, or until potatoes are tender.
Carefully remove foil and top with the shredded cheese. Return to oven to melt cheese.

Serves 6

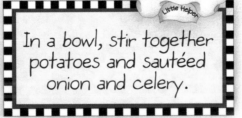

Little Helper

In a bowl, stir together potatoes and sautéed onion and celery.

Spuds au Gratin

7 medium-sized potatoes, peeled and quartered
6 tbsp unsalted butter
Salt and freshly ground black pepper, to taste
¼ tsp garlic powder
½ cup heavy cream (approximately)
½ cup grated Parmesan or Romano cheese
½ cup fine bread crumbs

Cook the potatoes in boiling water until tender. Drain and dry completely.

Preheat oven to 400° F.

Mash the potatoes. Add the butter, salt, pepper and garlic powder; blend well.

Blend in the cream a little at a time until you have the desired consistency. The mixture should not be too thin.

Spoon the potatoes into a shallow buttered baking dish.

Sprinkle the cheese and bread crumbs evenly over the potatoes.

Bake in oven until heated through and golden on top.

Serves 4

Sprinkle cheese and bread crumbs over potatoes.

Southwestern Refried Beans

2 (15-oz.) cans pinto beans
(without seasoning)
½ cup chopped onion
1 ½ tsp chili powder
1 clove garlic, minced
½ tsp salt
¼ tsp pepper
2 oz. Monterey Jack cheese
2 tbsp butter

In a large bowl, mash beans. Stir in all remaining ingredients, except butter.
In a large saucepan, melt the butter.
Add the bean mixture and slowly cook on low heat, stirring frequently, until beans have thickened.

Serves 4

French Green Bean Casserole

2 cans French-style green beans, drained
1 can cream of mushroom soup
1 can fried onion rings

Preheat oven to 350° F.
In a large bowl, mix together all ingredients with a spoon.
Pour mixture into a greased casserole dish.
Bake in oven for 1 hour.

Serves 4

Broccoli with Almond-Lemon Butter Sauce

1 pkg. frozen chopped broccoli, cooked
¼ cup butter
2 tbsp lemon juice
1 tsp grated lemon rind
¼ cup slivered almonds

Drain cooked broccoli and place in serving bowl.
In a saucepan, over low heat, melt the butter. Add the lemon juice, rind and almonds; heat for 1 minute.
Pour over hot broccoli and toss gently.
Serve immediately.

Serves 4-6

Zucchini Pancakes

2 cups shredded zucchini
2 tbsp chopped onion
2 tbsp all-purpose flour
¼ tsp salt
¼ tsp oregano
Dash of black pepper
1 tbsp chopped parsley
1 egg, beaten

In a small bowl, toss together the zucchini and onion.
Sprinkle with flour, salt, oregano, pepper and parsley. Mix with fork. Stir in egg.
Drop about ¼ cup batter per pancake into buttered skilled.
Cook over medium heat 2-3 minutes per side, or until golden brown and set.
Serve as a side dish.

Serves 4-6

Best Ever
Plain-ole' Peas

16-oz. pkg. black-eyed peas
6 cups water
4 slices hickory-smoked bacon
1 tbsp sugar
1 tbsp white vinegar
1 tbsp salt
¼ tsp black pepper
¼ tsp garlic salt

Sort and wash peas; place in a large Dutch oven. Cover with water 2 inches above peas; let soak 8 hours. Drain.
Add the 6 cups of water and remaining ingredients.
Bring to a boil. Cover, reduce heat and simmer for 1 ½ hours.

Makes 6 cups

Birthdays call for cakes – one-of-a-kind cakes, that is – and this makes me think of a very special cake prepared by a very special mom.

My older son's very first team sport was soccer. At the beginning of the season, the "Team Mom" would hand out snack schedules to all the parents. I, as most parents did when it was their turn, headed for the grocery store minutes before the game and tossed juice boxes and convenient portable snacks into the shopping cart before rushing off to the game. But there was one mom, Barb, who on her assigned day, would bring in lovingly and beautifully prepared baked goods and other mouth-watering snacks. Needless to say, she was quite a hit with the kids and the coaches.

We always celebrated the end of the fun-packed season with a team party. To top off the event, Barb entered the room carrying what looked to be a soccer ball covered with scrumptious icing and adorned with enough glowing candles to light up every face in the room. As all eyes opened wide and mouths started watering, she paraded the glowing marvel and placed it in the middle of the main table. I, as well as the other parents and kids, anxiously awaited my slice. Of course it tasted as good as it looked! To her credit, Barb was a single mom with three kids who also ran a local bakery. Barb and her kids were a treat to have on any team!

This chapter is chock-full of birthday party fare ideas, including an easy version of a Soccer Ball Cake, so that you can surprise your own little athlete.

Happy Birthday!

Banana Split Cake

Crust

2 cups vanilla wafers, crushed
½ cup sugar
½ cup butter or margarine, melted

Filling

16 oz. cream cheese, softened
1 cup sugar
1 tsp vanilla
3 large bananas, sliced
20 oz. crushed pineapple, well drained
12 oz. whipped topping
½ cup chopped nuts
4 oz. maraschino cherries, drained and halved

Preheat oven to 350° F.

Crust

In a large bowl, combine ½ cup sugar, crushed vanilla wafers and melted butter.
Press into a 9x13-inch pan.
Bake crust in oven for 15 minutes. Let cool.

Filling

In a mixing bowl, cream together cream cheese and sugar. Add vanilla.
Spread cream cheese mixture over vanilla wafer crust.
Continue layering with sliced bananas, pineapple, and whipped topping, in order.
Sprinkle with chopped nuts and then garnish with maraschino cherries.
Cover and refrigerate for 6 hours, or overnight.

Serves 8

Soccer Ball Cake

Cooking spray
2 tbsp all-purpose flour
¾ cup white sugar
Black food coloring
18-oz. pkg. yellow cake mix
16-oz. container vanilla frosting
12 black licorice whips

Preheat oven to 350° F.

Grease a 3-quart oven-proof bowl with cooking spray and dust with flour.
Place sugar in a small bowl and stir in a few drops of black food coloring, until desired color is achieved. Set aside.

Prepare cake batter according to package directions and pour into the prepared bowl. Bake for 1 hour and 15 minutes (or according to package directions). Let cake cool for 15 minutes in the bowl, then invert on plate and let cool completely. Once cake is completely cooled, trim flat side of cake and place on a cake board. Trim edges into a ball shape. Frost all over with vanilla frosting.

Next, using a toothpick, draw a pentagon in the center top of the cake. Surround the pentagon with five hexagons, repeating to cover entire cake. Cover lines with black licorice, cut into 1 ½-inch pieces.

Fill the pentagon shapes with black-colored sugar.
Let cake sit for 1 hour before serving.

Serves 6

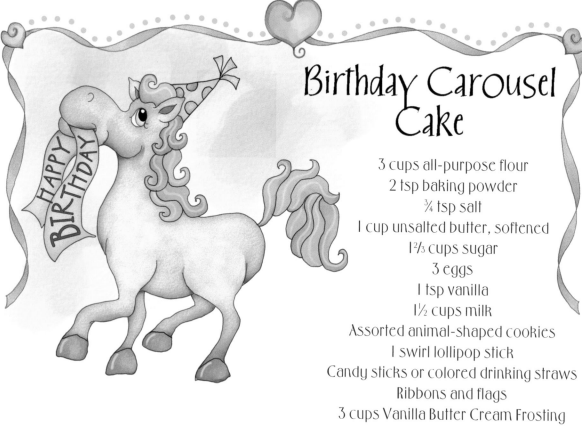

Birthday Carousel Cake

3 cups all-purpose flour
2 tsp baking powder
¾ tsp salt
1 cup unsalted butter, softened
1⅔ cups sugar
3 eggs
1 tsp vanilla
1½ cups milk
Assorted animal-shaped cookies
1 swirl lollipop stick
Candy sticks or colored drinking straws
Ribbons and flags
3 cups Vanilla Butter Cream Frosting
(recipe follows)

Preheat oven to 350° F.
Grease two 9x2-inch round cake pans.

In a medium size bowl, combine flour,
baking powder and salt.

In a separate bowl, beat together butter, sugar
and eggs until well blended. Beat in vanilla. Stir
in flour mixture and milk, mixing well.

Pour batter into 2 prepared pans, dividing equally.

Bake 25 to 30 minutes, or until a wooden toothpick
inserted in center comes out clean.

Cool cakes in pans for 5 minutes and then invert on wire rack to cool completely.

Vanilla Butter Cream Frosting

In a large bowl, beat together 2 cups powdered sugar, 1 cup softened unsalted butter, ½ cup heavy cream and 1½ tsp vanilla extract until smooth. Keep covered with plastic wrap until ready to use.

To assemble Carousel Cake, place one cake flat-side up on a serving plate.

Spread a thick layer (about 1 cup) of frosting over top.

Top with second cake layer, flat side down. Frost the entire cake with remaining frosting.

Insert lollipop in center of cake. Arrange candy sticks or drinking straws evenly around inside edge of cake.

Arrange animal cookies, flags and ribbons to resemble carousel.

Write "Happy Birthday" or child's name on flags. (Optional)

Serves 10-12

Kid Cool Fondue

2 pkg. instant chocolate pudding
2 pkg. instant vanilla pudding
2 pints strawberries
6 bananas
2 bunches green grapes
2 (8-oz.) bags shredded coconut
1 cup crushed almonds or peanuts
2 cups Cool Whip
(or real whipped cream, whipped)

Prepare chocolate and vanilla puddings according to package directions. Place in separate bowls and refrigerate while you prepare the rest of the recipe.

Wash and slice strawberries in half. Slice bananas into bite-size pieces. Wash grapes and place along with strawberries, bananas, coconut, nuts and Cool Whip in separate bowls for dipping.

Set the table with plates and forks.

Place the fruit, toppings and pudding bowls in the center of the table, with spoons for serving.

Place the fruit of your choice on your fork and dip into the pudding then the coconut and/or nuts and Cool Whip.

Serves 10-12

Little Helper

Set the table with plates and forks.

Barbie Doll Cake

Cooking spray
2 tbsp all-purpose flour
18-oz. pkg. white or yellow cake mix
2 (16-oz) containers vanilla frosting
1 drop food coloring

Preheat oven to 350° F.
Grease a 2-quart oven-proof glass mixing bowl with cooking spray and dust with flour.

Prepare cake according to package directions. Pour batter into prepared bowl. Bake 50-60 minutes, or until toothpick inserted into center comes out clean. Cool cake 15 minutes.

Invert on cake plate with widest part of cake on the bottom. Cool 3 hours before decorating.

Insert a clean Barbie doll into center of cake, up to her waist. Tint frosting with food coloring, making one or more colors.

Spread frosting evenly on the cake, making the doll's "skirt". Use a pastry bag with decorator tip to make the skirt as fancy as you like. Decorate the top of the doll, making the top of the dress.

Let sit for 1 hour before serving.

Serves 12

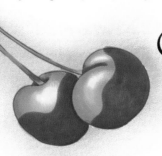

Choco-Cherry Cupcakes

24 whole maraschino cherries
1 pkg. chocolate chip cake mix
¼ cup cherry syrup
16 oz. chocolate frosting

- Preheat oven according to directions on cake mix box.
- Drain cherries; reserve syrup, pat dry.
- Prepare cake mix as directed on package, except substitute ¼ cup water for ¼ cup cherry syrup.
- Pour batter into cupcake tins and bake according to directions on cake box.
- Cool and frost cupcakes. Place a cherry in center of each cupcake.

Makes 24 cupcakes

Surprise Cupcakes

1 pkg. cake mix

Filling options	**Topping options**
maraschino cherries	cream cheese
almond, pecan, or walnut halves	pitted dates
candy kisses	raisins
chocolate mint wafers	frosting

- Preheat oven to 350° F. Grease cupcake tins.
- Prepare cake batter according to package directions.
- Spread 1 rounded tablespoon of batter into prepared tin cups.
- Place one of the fillings in the center of each cup.
- Top with an additional tablespoon of batter.
- Bake in oven for 25-30 minutes, or until golden brown.
- Remove cupcakes from tins; cool.
- Frost and decorate as desired.

Makes 24 cupcakes

Birthday Balloons

7 cups air-popped plain popcorn
¼ cup light corn syrup
1 tbsp margarine
1 tsp vanilla essence
¾ tsp cold water
1 cup confectioners' sugar
⅓ cup marshmallows
Food coloring of your (child's)
  favorite color
2-2 ½ yards colored string or ribbon,
  cut into 20 (3 to 5-inch) pieces

Place popcorn in a large bowl.

In a saucepan over medium heat, combine the corn syrup, margarine, vanilla, cold water, confectioners' sugar and marshmallows. Heat and stir until the mixture comes to a boil.

Stir in food coloring, adding one drop at a time, until desired color is reached.

Drizzle the hot mixture over the popcorn, coating each kernel evenly.

Grease hands with vegetable oil and quickly shape the coated popcorn into balls ("birthday balloons").

Attach one piece of string to each "balloon". Place on a large platter to serve.

Makes 15-20

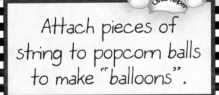

Little Helper

Attach pieces of string to popcorn balls to make "balloons".

Mini Hawaiian Beef Burgers

2 lbs. lean ground beef
2 tbsp ketchup
2 tbsp brown sugar
1 tsp pepper
1 tsp salt
1 clove garlic, finely minced
1 tsp onion powder
Mini hamburger buns (or large buns cut into ¼'s)
1 can small pineapple rings
Toppings of choice (ketchup, mustard, relish,
lettuce, tomato, pickle, etc.)

Preheat oven to 350° F.

In a medium bowl, mix together ground beef, ketchup, brown sugar, pepper, salt, garlic and onion powder. Work mixture with your hands, insuring that all ingredients are well incorporated.

Form meat into balls, a bit smaller than a golf ball. Flatten with your hands to create a burger patty shape.

Preheat your grill pan (or barbecue) to a high heat. Grill burgers until seared and grill marks appear, about 1 minute per side.

Transfer to baking sheet and finish cooking in the oven, about 5-10 minutes or until cooked through and no longer pink in the middle.

Place each burger on a mini hamburger bun. Top each with 1 pineapple ring and other toppings of your choice.

Makes 24

Honey-Baked Chicken Wings

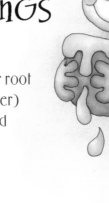

10 oz. soy sauce
2 tsp freshly grated ginger root
(or 1 tsp powdered ginger)
2 cloves garlic, minced
⅓ cup brown sugar
1 tsp honey mustard
24 chicken wings
Garlic powder
2 carrots
2 celery stalks

In a large bowl, mix together soy sauce, ginger, garlic, brown sugar and mustard; blend well. Marinate chicken wings in this mixture for at least 2 hours. Drain wings, reserving marinade.

Preheat oven to 350° F.

Place wings in baking dish and bake 1½ hours, turning and basting frequently. Discard any leftover marinade. Sprinkle baked wings with garlic powder and broil 1-2 minutes until crispy. Remove from oven and allow to cool while you prepare the vegetables.

Wash carrots and celery. Cut carrots in half lengthwise, then in half again. Cut across into 2-inch pieces, getting about 12 sticks from each whole carrot. Cut celery in half lengthwise, then in half again. Cut across into 2-inch pieces, getting about 12 sticks from each whole celery stalk.

Serve 4 carrot sticks and 4 celery sticks with 4 chicken wings.

Serves 6

BIRTHDAY PIZZA

1 pkg. active dry yeast
¾ cup lukewarm water
2 cups all-purpose flour
½ tsp salt
¼ tsp sugar
½ tbsp olive oil

In a small bowl, dissolve yeast in water; set aside for 5 minutes, stirring occasionally.

In a large bowl, combine flour, salt, sugar and oil; make a well in the center. When water/yeast mixture is bubbly, pour into center of well. Start kneading dough, bringing flour toward center of bowl; gradually increase kneading motion. If dough feels dry, add a little more water; if it feels sticky, add more flour. Knead vigorously until dough is smooth and elastic.

Roll into ball; cover with a damp cloth. Let rest for about 20 minutes at room temperature.

Beat dough with your palm to expel gas formed while fermenting. Roll dough again into ball; place in greased bowl. Baste with oil. Cover with plastic wrap; store in refrigerator.

When ready to use, place dough on floured counter top or table.
Flatten with your hands, working from center out (a rolling pin may do also).
Push dough evenly onto greased cookie sheet or pizza pan, forming a 12-inch circle with edges thicker than the middle.

TOPPINGS

½ - ¾ cup pizza sauce
½ red pepper, cut into long, thin strips
½ green pepper, cut into long, thin strips
1 cup shredded mozzarella cheese, loosely packed
½ yellow pepper, cut into long, thin strips
3-4 oz. pepperoni, sliced thin

Preheat oven to 450° F.

Place pizza dough on a 14-inch round non-stick baking pan. The edge will naturally be thicker but if not, roll the edge up a bit to make a thick crust. Spread sauce evenly on dough, right to the crust. Sprinkle cheese on top of sauce. Alternate peppers (red, then green, then yellow), around the rim of the pizza, where the sauce meets the crust, to make a colorful birthday border.

In the center of the pizza, make your child's birthday number using pepperoni slices. Use any leftover pepperoni slices and pepper strips to make birthday "balloons".

Bake in oven until crust is light brown and cheese begins to bubble, about 20 minutes. Remove the pizza from the oven and let it cool for 5-10 minutes. Place pizza on a cutting board and slice with a pizza cutter.

Makes 8 large or 16 small slices

Make birthday "balloons" using pepperoni and pepper strips.

Chicken Nuggets

1 lb. boneless chicken tenders
Vegetable oil for deep frying
⅓ cup all-purpose flour
¼ tsp salt
1½ tsp vinegar
¼ tsp baking soda
⅓ cup water

Cut chicken into nugget-size pieces, about 1x ½-inch.

Put oil in deep fryer and heat to 360° F.

In a large bowl, mix together flour and salt.

In a separate small bowl, mix vinegar with baking soda. Add vinegar mixture and water to the flour mixture; beat until smooth.

Dip chicken pieces into batter, allowing excess batter to drip off into the bowl.

Fry chicken nuggets, 4 to 6 at a time, until golden brown, or about 4 minutes for each batch.

Drain on paper towels.

Serves 8

Sausage Balls

1 lb. hot sausage, crumbled
1 lb. mild sausage, crumbled
12 oz. sharp cheese, softened
12 oz. mild cheese, softened
4 cups Bisquick

Preheat oven to 400° F.
In a large bowl, mix together all ingredients until well combined.
Roll mixture into small balls. Place balls on cookie sheets.
Bake in oven for 10 minutes.
Serve warm.

Makes 20-30

Piggly-Wigglies

1 tube refrigerated crescent rolls
8 slices Cheddar cheese
8 frankfurters

Preheat oven to 350° F.
Separate dough into 8 triangles.
Wrap a cheese slice around each frank and
then a crescent roll triangle around both.
Place on an ungreased cookie sheet.
Bake 10-13 minutes, or until crescent rolls
are nicely browned.

Serves 8

Broccoli-Cheese Squares

3 tbsp butter
2 (10-oz.) pkg. frozen chopped broccoli
3 large eggs
1 cup milk
1 cup all-purpose flour
1 tsp baking powder
1 tsp salt
4 cups coarsely shredded mild Cheddar cheese
2 tbsp finely chopped onion
Seasoned salt

Preheat oven to 350° F. Grease a 9x13-inch baking dish with the butter.

Steam broccoli until partially cooked, about 3 minutes. Cool and pat dry with paper towels.

In a large bowl, beat eggs and milk until frothy.

In a separate bowl, mix together flour, baking powder and salt; stir into egg mixture, mixing well. Fold in broccoli, cheese and onion.

Spoon into baking dish, spreading evenly. Sprinkle with seasoned salt.

Bake in oven about 35 minutes, or until set and lightly browned. Let stand 5 minutes, then cut into bite-size pieces.

Makes 4 dozen 1½-inch squares

Crispy Ravioli

2 large eggs, beaten
2 tbsp milk
Salt and freshly ground pepper to taste
2 cups bread crumbs
Vegetable oil for deep frying
1 pkg. frozen cheese ravioli, thawed
(about 3 dozen)
¼ cup Parmesan cheese (optional)
26-28-oz. jar marinara sauce, heated

In a large bowl, whisk together the eggs, milk, salt and pepper.

Place bread crumbs in a separate large bowl or large dish.

Heat oil in a deep pan over medium high heat or in a deep fryer heated to 300° F. Dip ravioli into egg mixture and then coat with bread crumbs. Fry about 6 to 8 ravioli at a time until golden brown. Drain on paper towels.

If desired, sprinkle with Parmesan cheese while still hot.
Serve with warm marinara sauce for dipping.

Serves 4-6

Little Helper

Measure out bread crumbs and place in large dish.

Cherry Dot Squares

2 cans (20) refrigerated biscuits
3 eggs
1 small can evaporated milk
½ cup sugar
1 tsp vanilla
¼ cup margarine
21-oz. can apple pie filling
1 tsp cinnamon
1 cup water
12 cherries, pitted

Preheat oven to 350° F.

Bake biscuits according to package directions and allow to cool.

In a large mixing bowl, break biscuits into quarters.

Add eggs, milk, sugar, vanilla, margarine, pie filling, cinnamon and water to biscuits. Mix well.

Pour mixture into a 9x12-inch cake pan, coated with cooking spray. Spread batter evenly.

Place cherries evenly spaced on top of mixture.

Bake in oven for 30-40 minutes, or until toothpick inserted in center comes out clean.

Cool and cut into squares.

Makes 12 squares!

Apple Rice Parfait

1 pkg. vanilla pudding mix (not instant)
2½ cups milk
3 ½ cups cooked rice
½ cup sour cream
½ tsp ground cinnamon
⅛ tsp ground nutmeg
1 can apple pie filling
⅓ cup raisins
1½ tsp lemon juice
Ground cinnamon

Prepare pudding according to package directions using 2½ cups milk. Remove from heat and fold in cooked rice, sour cream, ½ tsp cinnamon and nutmeg into hot pudding; set aside.

In a large bowl, combine apple pie filling, raisins and lemon juice; mix well.

Spoon about ⅓ cup of the pudding into 8 parfait or dessert dishes; top with about ¼ cup of the apple mixture. Spoon remaining pudding on top of apple mixture. Sprinkle with cinnamon, if desired.

Serve warm or chilled.

Serves 8

CARAMEL APPLE DIP

3 (8-oz.) pkg. cream cheese
1½ cups brown sugar
3 tbsp vanilla extract
6 green apples

In a large mixing bowl, combine cream cheese, brown sugar and vanilla; mix well. (If the mixture is too runny for your taste, add a small amount of brown sugar to the mixture. If the mixture is too thick for your taste, add a small amount of vanilla extract.)

Keep sauce at room temperature until ready to serve.

Cut each apple into 16 slices.
Serve 8 apple slices (½ an apple) with
¼ cup caramel sauce for dipping.

Serves 12

Chocolate-Dipped Goodies

4 squares semi-sweet chocolate
Any combination of the following:
marshmallows
pretzels
strawberries
banana slices
pineapple chunks (fresh or canned)
orange slices
maraschino cherries
figs, dates or apricots

In a saucepan, melt the chocolate over very low heat, stirring constantly until smooth. Use wooden picks, skewers, or a fork to dip above items into chocolate, one at a time.

Let stand on rack or waxed paper until chocolate is firm. Chill.

Best when served the same day.

Makes 1 to 1 ½ dozen

Sweet Party Mix

12-oz. pkg. crispy corn and rice cereal
5 oz. slivered almonds
6 oz. toasted chopped pecans
¾ cup butter
¾ cup corn syrup
1½ cups light brown sugar

Preheat oven to 250° F. Lightly grease a large roasting pan.

In a large bowl, mix together crispy corn and rice cereal, almonds and pecans.

In a medium saucepan over medium heat, melt the butter and add the corn syrup and brown sugar, stirring until well blended.

Pour the liquid over the cereal/nut mixture in bowl; stir and shake until all the nuts and cereal are well coated.

Pour the coated mixture into the prepared roasting pan. Bake 1 hour in preheated oven, stirring every 15 minutes, or so.

Cool on wax paper and store in airtight container.

Serves 20-24

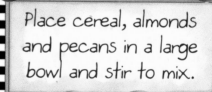

Place cereal, almonds and pecans in a large bowl and stir to mix.

Chocolate Peanut Popcorn

2 quarts unsalted popped popcorn
1 cup miniature marshmallows
½ cup salted peanuts
9 (3/4-oz.) bars milk chocolate

Preheat oven to 300° F.
Spread popped popcorn on a buttered baking sheet.
Sprinkle with marshmallows and peanuts.
Arrange chocolate bars over the top.
Heat in oven for 5 minutes. Cool slightly and toss.

Makes 2½ quarts

Orange Blush

2 (6-oz.) cans frozen orange juice
   concentrate, thawed
2 cups cranberry juice cocktail
½ cup sugar
28-oz. bottle club soda, chilled
Crushed ice

In a serving pitcher, combine orange juice concentrate, cranberry juice cocktail and sugar; stir well to dissolve sugar. Chill thoroughly.
Stir in chilled club soda just before serving.
Pour over crushed ice in glasses and serve.

Makes 8 cups

Each and every year that my boys were in elementary school, I would look forward to assisting in holiday classroom celebrations. School hallways would be decorated with drawings of snowmen, whimsical Santas and angels in flight. Colorful paper-link garlands were draped across the bulletin boards. Teachers and staff would dress up in red and green while they shepherded their flocks of rambunctious students.

A highlight of the holiday agenda would be the construction of Gingerbread Houses. Students would be divided up into small groups and enough supplies of brightly-colored holiday candy and small fruits would be passed out for building and decorating the elaborate gingerbread homes. It was always amazing to see the diverse versions that would grace the tables by the end of the day. And what looks of pride and accomplishment would be on each little builder's face! The completed houses would be carefully picked up and placed on appointed spots by the window so that they could be admired for the rest of the holiday season.

Have fun constructing your own gingerbread house with your kids. You will be surprised at their many creative ideas!

Merry Christmas!

Roast Goose with Stuffing and Gravy

Stuffing
10 (1-inch thick) slices French bread, cut into cubes
1 cup dried currants
4 apples, peeled, cored and sliced
1 tbsp dried thyme
4 tbsp butter or margarine, melted

10-lb. goose
1 tbsp vegetable oil
1 onion, chopped
1 carrot, chopped
1 stalk celery, chopped
1 clove garlic, minced
1 sprig fresh thyme
1 sprig fresh marjoram
¼ cup white wine
1 tsp tomato paste
10 ½-oz. can condensed chicken broth
Salt to taste
Ground black pepper to taste
1 tbsp cornstarch (optional)
¼ cup water (optional)

To make stuffing, in a large bowl, combine bread cubes, currants, apples, crumbled thyme, salt, pepper and melted butter or margarine.

Wash goose inside and out; pat dry. Stuff, truss, and tie goose. Prick bird all over with fork.

Preheat oven to 375° F.

Heat oil in roasting pan on top of stove. Brown goose lightly on all sides, and then drain off pan drippings.

Set goose breast side up in roasting pan. Add a little water, cover, and roast for one hour. Discard fat from roasting pan.

In a mixing bowl, combine chopped onion, carrot, celery, garlic, fresh thyme and marjoram and arrange mixture around goose. Continue roasting, uncovered, for 20 to 25 minutes per pound (3 to 3½ hours). Drain off fat every 45 minutes, adding more water as required.

Transfer cooked goose to platter and keep warm by covering loosely with foil. Skim off remaining fat in pan and heat drippings and vegetables on top of stove until mixture is reduced. Stir in white wine, tomato paste, chicken broth and seasonings; simmer for 10-15 minutes, then strain. If necessary, add a little cornstarch mixed with water to thicken gravy.

Serves 6-8

Little Helper

Wash goose inside and out; pat dry with paper towels.

Turkey Cheese Puffs

3-oz. pkg. cream cheese, softened
2 tbsp butter or margarine, softened
2 tbsp milk
2 cups chopped cooked turkey
1/8 tsp pepper
8-oz. can refrigerated crescent dinner rolls

Preheat oven to 350° F.

In a large bowl, combine cream cheese and butter and beat at medium speed with an electric mixer until smooth. Add milk and continue beating until smooth. Remove bowl from mixer and stir in the turkey and pepper.

Open the can and unroll refrigerated dinner rolls. Separate the dough into 4 rectangles. Press and smooth the perforations between the triangles to create a smooth rectangle. Spoon ½ cup of the turkey mixture into the center of each rectangle.

Moisten the edges of each rectangle with a little water. Bring the 4 corners to the center over the filling. Pinch the edges together to seal.

Place the turkey-cheese puffs on an ungreased baking sheet. Bake for 20 to 25 minutes, or until golden.

Serves 4

Note: Great way to use up leftover roast turkey.

Christmas Salad

1½ cups chopped fresh cranberries
1 cup chopped red apple
1 cup chopped celery
1 cup seedless green grapes, halved
¼ cup chopped walnuts
1 tbsp white sugar
¼ tsp ground cinnamon
½ cup vanilla yogurt
½ cup plain yogurt

Chop cranberries in a food processor. Prepare all other ingredients.
In a large bowl, combine cranberries, apple, celery, grapes, walnuts, sugar, cinnamon, and yogurts. Toss to coat evenly.
Cover and chill 2 hours. Stir just before serving.

Serves 4-6

Asparagus au Gratin

2 tbsp butter
2 tbsp all-purpose flour
1 cup milk
½ tsp salt
1 cup grated Cheddar cheese

1 cup soft bread crumbs
1 can asparagus, drained
2 hard-boiled eggs, sliced
½ cup chopped pimiento

Preheat oven to 350° F.
In medium saucepan, melt butter; stir in flour. Stir in milk and salt; cook until thickened, stirring constantly. Add cheese; stir until melted.
Sprinkle half the bread crumbs in bottom of casserole dish. Arrange asparagus and eggs in dish; add pimiento. Cover with cheese sauce; top with remaining crumbs.
Bake in oven for 45 minutes.

Serves 4

Garlic Mashed Potatoes and Yams

4 cloves garlic
1 tbsp olive oil
1½ lbs. Yukon Gold potatoes, peeled and cubed
1½ lbs. yams, peeled and cubed
½ cup milk
¼ cup butter
¼ tsp rosemary
Salt and pepper to taste

Preheat oven to 350° F. Lightly grease an 8-inch square baking dish; set aside.

Place garlic in small oven-proof dish and drizzle with olive oil; roast for 30 minutes, or until very soft. Cool and peel the garlic over a small bowl to reserve the oil.

In a large pot of salted water, boil potatoes and yams until tender, about 20 minutes; drain, reserving 1 cup liquid.

Place potatoes and yams in a large bowl with milk, butter, rosemary, roasted garlic and reserved olive oil. Mash to desired consistency, adding reserved cooking liquid as needed. Season with salt and pepper to taste.

Transfer to prepared baking dish and bake until heated through and golden on top, about 45 minutes.

Serves 8

Cola Pot Roast with Potatoes and Carrots

1 sirloin tip roast (about 4 lbs.)
¼ cup cooking oil
Garlic powder
1 envelope Lipton Onion Soup mix
1 can cream of mushroom soup
2 (12-oz.) cans of cola
2 cups water
6 medium potatoes, peeled and cut in half
6 carrots, cut in 2-inch pieces

Preheat oven to 350° F.

In large frying pan or skillet, brown roast on both sides in ¼ cup of hot cooking oil. After browning, sprinkle roast with garlic powder and transfer to roasting pan. Add remaining ingredients, except vegetables. Cover and cook for about 3 hours.

Thirty minutes before roast is done, add potatoes and carrots and 2 cups more water. Cook until vegetables are tender.

Serves 4-6

Baked Pineapple Ham

7-8-lb. ham
1 can (15 oz.) pineapple slices with juice
¼ cup light brown sugar
¼ cup honey
2 tbsp lemon juice
Whole cloves

Preheat oven to 325° F.

Place ham, uncovered, in roasting pan, fat side up. Cover loosely with aluminum foil; bake in oven for about 2 ½ hours, or 20 minutes per pound.

Drain pineapple, reserving ½ cup of juice. Combine the reserved juice, brown sugar, honey and lemon juice in a saucepan; cook over low heat until sugar is dissolved, stirring occasionally.

About 45 minutes before ham has finished baking, remove from oven. Remove foil from ham; skin and score fat and dot with whole cloves. Brush ham with pineapple-honey mixture.

Arrange pineapple slices over the top of the ham, securing with toothpicks. Brush again with pineapple-honey mixture.

Bake an additional 45 minutes at 325° F, basting with pineapple-honey mixture from time to time.

Serves 10-12

Drain pineapple slices from can and measure out ½ cup of juice.

Tourtière (Meat Pie)

1 lb. lean ground beef or veal
1 lb. lean ground pork
1 large onion, minced
1 stalk celery (diced fine)
1 large baking potato (cut in small cubes)
½ tsp garlic
¼ tsp ground cloves
1 dash ground allspice
½ tsp ground cinnamon
1 tsp sage
½ tsp salt
½ tsp ground black pepper
24 oz. beef bouillon
Pastry for 2 two-crust pies (4 shells)

In large pot, brown ground meats; drain off excess fat. Add onion, celery, potato, garlic, cloves, allspice, cinnamon, sage, salt and pepper and mix well. Add bouillon, bring to a boil and then simmer on low heat for 2-3 hours. Drain off excess liquid; cool meat mixture.

Preheat oven to 350° F.

Fill two shells with ½ the meat mixture each, cover with top crusts, seal edges and slit top crusts a few times to allow steam to escape. Bake in oven for approximately 45 minutes, or until the crusts are golden brown.

Serves 8-10

Note: This is a popular French-Canadian traditional Christmas recipe.

Gingerbread House

¾ cup butter
½ cup brown sugar
¼ cup white sugar
1½ tbsp lemon juice
½ cup molasses

2 eggs
3 cups all-purpose flour
2 tsp baking powder
1 tbsp ground ginger
2 tsp ground allspice

Icing

6 egg whites
4 (16-oz.) pkg. confectioners' sugar, sifted
Assorted candy pieces for decoration

First, cut out in thin cardboard: a side wall, 5x8 inches; an end wall, 5x5 inches; a triangular gable, 5x3x3 inches; a roof rectangle, 4x9 inches; a chimney, front: 2½ x 1 inch, back: 1½ x 1 inch, side: 2½ x 1 inch (trim). Tape the rectangular end wall piece to the triangular gable piece: match the long side (5 inches) of the triangle to one side of the end wall.

In a large bowl, cream together butter and both sugars until light and fluffy. Stir in lemon juice and molasses. Gradually beat in 2 eggs. Sift the flour, baking powder and spices together; stir into creamed mixture. Cover and refrigerate for 1 hour.

Preheat oven to 375° F. On a floured surface, roll out the dough to ¼-inch thickness. Place the cardboard pattern pieces on the dough and cut around the edges. Cut out two of each. Gently, using a spatula, lift the dough and place it on greased baking trays.

Bake gingerbread in oven for 10 minutes, or until crisp. Leave the gingerbread on the baking trays for a few minutes to set, and then transfer to wire racks. Leave out overnight to harden.

In a large bowl, lightly whisk 2 egg whites. Gradually beat in approximately 4 cups confectioners' sugar. The icing should be smooth and stand in firm peaks.

Pipe a 9-inch line of icing onto a cake board, and press in one of the side walls so that it sticks firmly and stands upright. Take an end wall and ice both the side edges. Pipe a line of icing on the board at a right angle to the first wall, and press the end wall into position. Repeat this process with the other two walls until they are all in position. Let the roofless house dry for at least 2 hours until the icing is firmly set. Pipe a thick layer of icing on top of all the walls, and fix the roof pieces in position; the roof should overlap the walls to make the eaves. Pipe a little icing along the crest of the roof to hold the two pieces firmly together. Let dry for half an hour.

To attach the chimney, on one side of the roof near the peak, glue one angled piece to the roof with icing. Glue the largest rectangle to the angled piece and then glue the second angled piece in place. Last, glue the smallest rectangle. Hide any mistakes under a "snow" of icing.

Let the house dry until completely solid, preferably overnight. When ready to decorate, make the remaining icing. In a large bowl, lightly whisk 4 egg whites, and mix in remaining confectioners' sugar as before. Use this to make snow on the roof, and to stick on various candies in any way you like!

Snowballs

1 cup butter
½ cup confectioners' sugar
1 tsp vanilla extract
2 cups sifted all-purpose flour
1 cup finely chopped pecans
¼ tsp salt
½ cup confectioners' sugar for decoration
Colored sugar sprinkles (optional)

Preheat oven to 350° F.

In a large bowl, cream butter with ½ cup of the confectioners' sugar and the vanilla. Add flour, nuts and salt; mix well. Shape dough into 1-inch balls and place on ungreased baking sheet. Bake for 12 to 15 minutes. Do not allow cookies to get too brown. While cookies are still hot, roll them in confectioners' sugar, and then in colored sprinkles, if desired.

Makes 4 dozen

White Chocolate and Cranberry Cookies

½ cup butter, softened
½ cup packed brown sugar
½ cup white sugar
1 egg
1 tbsp vanilla

1½ cups all-purpose flour
½ tsp baking soda
¾ cup white chocolate chips
1 cup dried cranberries

Preheat oven to 375° F. Grease cookie sheets.

In a large bowl, cream together the butter and both sugars until smooth. Beat in the egg and vanilla. Combine the flour and baking soda; stir into the sugar mixture.

Stir in the white chocolate chips and cranberries. Drop by heaping spoonfuls onto prepared cookie sheets. Bake in oven for 8 to 10 minutes. Allow cookies to cool for 1 minute on cookie sheets before transferring to wire racks to cool completely.

Makes 2 dozen

Christmas Wreath Cookies

½ cup unsalted butter
4 cups miniature marshmallows
(or 40 large marshmallows)
1½ tsp liquid green food coloring
½ tsp almond extract
½ tsp vanilla extract
4 cups corn flakes
1 pkg. (2¼ oz.) red hot candies

In 2-quart saucepan, melt butter over medium-low heat; add marshmallows, stirring constantly, until smooth. Quickly mix in the food coloring, almond and vanilla extracts. Add the cornflakes and stir until well coated.

Drop by heaping tablespoonfuls onto waxed paper or aluminum foil sprayed with non-stick cooking spray. Work quickly to keep the mixture from hardening before it is shaped. With buttered fingers, quickly shape mixture into wreaths.

Decorate with red hot candies.

Once the wreaths dry, you may string them with nylon string or gold ribbon and use them as tree ornaments.

Makes 3 dozen

Christmas Fruitcake

4 cups all-purpose flour
1½ tsp ground cinnamon
1 tsp ground nutmeg
½ tsp ground cloves
1 tsp baking powder
½ tsp salt
1 cup butter or margarine, softened
1½ cups brown sugar, firmly packed
5 eggs, separated
½ cup molasses
½ cup milk
2 cups chopped candied red and green cherries
½ cup chopped citron
1 cup chopped raisins
1 cup chopped dates
1 cup chopped walnuts

Preheat oven to 325° F.

Grease two 9x5x3-inch loaf pans or two 6-cup fluted tube pans.

Sift the flour with cinnamon, nutmeg, cloves, baking powder and salt.

In a large mixing bowl, at medium speed, cream together butter and sugar until light and fluffy. Add the egg yolks, one at a time, beating well. Stir in molasses and milk. Add the flour/spice mixture, a little at a time, beating well after each addition.

In a separate bowl, with a clean beater, beat the egg whites until stiff; gently fold them into the batter. Add the fruit and nuts and stir in by hand until all ingredients are well mixed.

Pour batter into prepared pans, dividing equally.

Bake 1 hour for tube cake pans; 65 to 70 minutes for loaf pans. (Test for doneness with toothpick inserted in center of cakes.) Cool cakes in pans for 15 minutes. Unmold cakes onto wire racks to cool completely.

When cakes are cooled, drizzle with Bourbon Glaze, if desired.

Bourbon Glaze

Whisk together 1 cup powdered sugar, 1 tbsp bourbon and 1 tbsp butter in a small bowl. Gradually whisk in 2 tbsp hot water.

Serves 10-12

Chocolate Pecan Pie

2 eggs
½ cup unsifted all-purpose flour
½ cup sugar
½ cup brown sugar
1 cup butter, melted and cooled
6-oz. pkg. chocolate chips (1 cup)
1 cup chopped pecans
2 (δ-inch) pie shells, unbaked

Preheat oven to 325° F.
In a large mixing bowl, beat eggs until foamy.
Beat in the flour, sugar and brown sugar until well blended.
Blend in melted butter.
Stir in chocolate chips and pecans.
Pour into pie shells and bake in oven for 1 hour.

Makes 2 pies

Christmas Eggnog

6 large eggs, separated
¾ cup sugar
½ cup brandy *
¼ cup rum *
4 cups milk
4 cups cream
Dash vanilla to taste
½ cup icing sugar
Nutmeg for sprinkling

In a large bowl, beat the yolks; gradually beat in the sugar until well blended. Slowly beat in the brandy and rum; add the milk and half of the cream. Keep chilled until ready to use.
Just before serving, beat the egg whites until stiff and fold them into the eggnog mixture. Add the vanilla.
Whip together the remaining cream and icing sugar until thick.
Top each glass of eggnog with whipped cream and a dash of nutmeg.

Serves δ

*Note: For non-alcoholic eggnog, replace brandy and rum with ¾ cup milk.

Candy Cane Cookies

1 cup butter, softened
1 cup confectioners' sugar
1 egg
½ cup milk
1 tsp vanilla
½ tsp peppermint extract
2½ cups sifted all-purpose flour
½ tsp salt
1 tsp baking soda
2 tbsp red food coloring

In a large bowl, cream together the butter and sugar until light and fluffy. Beat in egg, milk, vanilla and peppermint extract.

In a separate bowl, mix together flour, salt and baking soda. Stir into the sugar mixture. Divide the dough in half and incorporate the red food coloring to half the dough. Refrigerate dough for one hour.

Preheat the oven to 375° F.

Take one teaspoon of each color of dough and roll out into 4-inch long strips on floured surface. Lay the strips side by side and twist together to make a red and white striped rope.

Place the dough ropes on an ungreased cookie sheet. (Place the canes 1 inch apart.) Turn the end into a curve to make the cane's handle. Bake in oven for 9 to 12 minutes. Cool on the cookie sheet for 5 minutes, then transfer to wire rack to cool completely.

Makes 1 dozen

Gingerbread Cut-Outs

4 cups all-purpose flour
½ tsp baking soda
½ tsp salt
½ tsp ground allspice
½ tsp ground cloves
½ tsp ground cinnamon
½ tsp ground ginger
½ cup softened butter or margarine
½ cup brown sugar
⅓ cup molasses
2 eggs
Raisins, chocolate chips, candy pieces,
frosting, etc. for decoration

Preheat oven to 350° F.

In a bowl, combine the flour, baking soda, salt, allspice, cloves, cinnamon and ginger; set aside.

In a large bowl, cream together the butter and brown sugar until smooth. Stir in the molasses and eggs. Add the flour mixture; stir to form a stiff dough. Divide dough into 2 pieces.

On a lightly floured surface, roll out the dough to ⅛-inch thickness. Cut into desired shapes using cookie cutters. Place cookies, 1 inch apart, on ungreased cookie sheets.

Bake in preheated oven for 8 to 10 minutes. Allow cookies to cool on baking sheet for 5 minutes before removing to a wire rack to cool completely.

Decorate cookies with frosting, raisins, chocolate chips, or candy pieces.

Use your favorite cookie cutters to cut out shapes. Have fun decorating the cooled cookies.

There is just something about pumpkins that lets you know the holiday season is just around the corner. Come late autumn, our neighborhood grocery store always creates a display of pumpkins across the front of the store, interspersed with beautiful fall mums. On entering the store you are greeted with the sweet smell of pumpkin pies being baked. There is no way to resist coming out of there without at least one pumpkin delicacy purchase.

One of my favorite things to bake during the holidays is pumpkin bread. The smell of warm cinnamon and nutmeg has always enticed my kids into the kitchen to await the emergence from the oven of this scrumptious goody. I always bake two pumpkin breads at a time so that I am assured of getting at least one piece myself!

Holiday Specials

Holiday Pork Roast

5-lb. bone-in pork roast
8 cloves garlic, peeled and halved
¼ cup water
3 tbsp brown sugar
10-oz. jar maraschino cherries, with juice
Oven bag

Preheat the oven to 350° F.

Rinse and pat dry the pork roast. Cut deep slits all over the roast with a sharp knife to different depths. Press pieces of garlic into the slits.

In a small bowl, mix together the water, brown sugar and the maraschino cherries with their juice.

Place the roast in an oven bag, and pour the cherry mixture over. Seal the bag and place in a roasting pan.

Bake for 3 hours, or until the internal temperature of the roast is at least 160° F.

Remove roast from bag to a serving plate; baste with the juices.

Let stand for 15 minutes before carving and serving.

Serves 6-8

Classic Roast Turkey

12-lb. whole turkey
¾ cup olive oil
2 tbsp garlic powder
1 tsp salt
½ tsp black pepper
1¼ quarts turkey stock

Preheat oven to 325° F.

Remove the turkey neck and giblets, rinse the turkey and pat dry with paper towels. Place the turkey, breast side up, on a rack in a roasting pan.

In a small bowl, combine olive oil, garlic powder, salt and black pepper. Brush turkey with olive oil mixture.

Pour 2 cups turkey stock into the bottom of the roasting pan and cover turkey with an aluminum foil tent.

Baste all over every 30 minutes with juices from bottom of pan. Whenever drippings evaporate, add stock to moisten, about 1 to 2 cups at a time.

Bake for 3 to 3½ hours, or until the internal temperature of the thickest part of the thigh measures 180° F.

Remove from oven and allow to stand for about 30 minutes before carving.

Serves 12-16

Turkey Pot Pie

1 pkg. (10 oz.) frozen peas and carrots
2 tbsp butter
2 tbsp flour
⅓ cup chopped onion
½ tsp salt
¼ tsp pepper
1¾ cup chicken broth
⅔ cup milk
2 cups diced cooked turkey
1 small potato, cooked and diced
Pastry for 9-inch two-crust pie

Preheat oven to 375° F.

Rinse frozen peas and carrots in cold water to separate; drain and set aside.

Melt butter in 2-quart saucepan over medium heat. Add flour, onion, salt and pepper. Cook, stirring constantly, until mixture is bubbly. Stir in broth and milk. Bring to a boil over medium heat, stirring constantly, and continue boiling for 1 minute. Stir in turkey, peas and carrots and potato.

Remove from heat, pour mixture into pie crust. Cover with top crust; seal and flute edges. Cut several slits in top crust.

Bake in oven for about 35 minutes, or until crust is golden brown.

Serves 4-6

Note: Makes good use of leftover roast turkey.

Little Helper

Rinse frozen peas and carrots in cold water to separate pieces; drain well.

Mexican Corn Bread

2 cups self-rising cornmeal flour
3 eggs, beaten
1 cup buttermilk
1 large onion, chopped
1 green bell pepper, chopped
1 red bell pepper, chopped
1 cup shredded Cheddar cheese
Hot pepper sauce, to taste
1 can cream-style corn

Preheat oven to 350° F.
In a large bowl, mix together all ingredients until well blended.
Pour into greased muffin tins. Bake in oven for 45 minutes.

Makes 18 muffins

Cinnamon-Butter Carrots

9 small carrots, scraped
3 tbsp butter, melted
¼ cup brown sugar
½ tsp salt
¼ tsp cinnamon
3 tbsp boiling water

Preheat oven to 350°F.
Place carrots in a 1-quart casserole baking dish.
In a small bowl, combine the butter, sugar, salt, cinnamon and water. Pour over carrots.
Cover and bake in oven for 1¼ hours, or until carrots are tender.

Serves 4

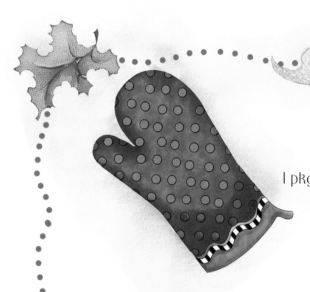

Dilly Beans

6 cups water
1 pkg. (14-oz.) frozen whole green beans, thawed
2 tbsp extra virgin olive oil
2 tbsp cider vinegar
¼ cup finely chopped green onions
2 tbsp chopped fresh dill
¼ tsp salt
¼ tsp black pepper

In a large saucepan, bring water to a boil; add green beans and cook about
10 minutes, or until tender.
In a small bowl, whisk together olive oil, vinegar, green onions, dill, salt and pepper.
Drain cooked beans well and place in serving dish.
Drizzle dill sauce over the beans and toss gently to coat well.

Serves 6-8

Potato and Herb Wedges

7 or 8 red new potatoes
Olive oil
2 cloves garlic, finely minced
½ tsp salt
½ tsp black pepper
2 tbsp Herbes de Provence

Preheat oven to 350° F.
Wash potatoes and cut into quarters. Place potatoes into a 13x9x2-inch baking pan.
Drizzle enough olive oil over potatoes to lightly coat.
Sprinkle minced garlic, salt, black pepper and Herbes de Provence over potatoes
and toss. Bake in oven for 1 hour.

Serves 4-6

Creamy Baked Squash

1½ lbs. squash or pumpkin, cubed
1 tbsp olive oil
1½ cups chopped yellow onions
1 tsp salt
3 medium cloves garlic, minced
½ tsp black pepper
¼ tsp cayenne pepper
½ cup firm plain yogurt
1 cup cottage cheese

Place squash in a medium soup pot and cover with water. Cook over medium heat until soft, about 20 minutes.

Preheat oven to 375° F.

Place cooked squash in a large bowl and mash well.

Heat olive oil in a medium-sized frying pan. Add onions and salt; sauté over medium heat until onions are soft and lightly browned, about 5 minutes.

Add garlic, black pepper and cayenne; sauté for another 2-3 minutes.

Add the onion sauté, along with yogurt and cottage cheese to the squash; mix well.

Spread mixture into an ungreased 9-inch square baking dish.

Bake uncovered for 25-30 minutes, or until bubbly.

Serves 5

Use a potato masher to mash cooked squash well.

Sour Cream Apple Pie

¾ cup sugar
2 tbsp all-purpose flour
1 cup sour cream
1 egg
½ tsp vanilla
⅛ tsp salt
2 cups thinly sliced tart apples
1 pie shell, unbaked

Topping
⅓ cup sugar
1 tsp cinnamon
⅓ cup all-purpose flour
¼ cup butter

Preheat oven to 425° F.

In a large bowl, combine sugar and flour. Mix in the sour cream, egg, vanilla and salt. Fold in the apples and pour mixture into the unbaked pie shell.

Bake in oven for 20 minutes.

To prepare topping, combine first 3 ingredients in a medium-size bowl. Cut in the butter and sprinkle over pie.

Reduce oven temperature to 325° F. and continue baking pie for another 20 minutes.

Serves 6-8

Sweet Potato Crunch

6 sweet potatoes
1 cup sugar
⅓ cup well-packed brown sugar
2 eggs
1 stick butter, softened
1 tsp vanilla extract
1 tsp nutmeg
1 tsp cinnamon

Crunch Topping
⅓ cup melted butter
⅓ cup all-purpose flour
1 cup brown sugar
1 cup chopped pecans
1 tbsp cinnamon

Boil sweet potatoes until tender.

Preheat oven to 350° F.

When boiled potatoes are cooled, remove skins and place in a large mixing bowl. Whip potatoes until fluffy, adding the next 7 ingredients.

Spread potato mixture into a buttered casserole dish and top with the crunch topping mixture.

Bake in oven for 45 minutes.

Serves 4-6

Autumn Pumpkin Pie

1¼ cups pumpkin purée
¼ cup brown sugar
½ cup sugar
½ tsp salt
¼ tsp ground ginger
1 tsp ground cinnamon
½ tsp ground nutmeg
1 tsp all-purpose flour
2 eggs, beaten
1 cup unsweetened condensed milk
2 tbsp water
½ tsp vanilla extract
1 unbaked 9-inch single crust pie shell

Preheat oven to 400° F.

In a large bowl, mix together pumpkin purée, both sugars, salt, spices and flour.
Add eggs; mix well to combine.
Add condensed milk, water and vanilla; mix well.

Pour into pastry-lined pie pan.
Bake in preheated oven for 15 minutes.
Reduce heat to 350° F. and bake about 35 minutes more, or until center is set.

Serves 8

Pumpkin Muffins

2 cups all-purpose flour
2 tsp baking powder
1 tsp baking soda
2 tsp ground cinnamon
2 tsp ground nutmeg
2 eggs, beaten
1 cup pumpkin purée
¾ cup sugar
2 cups unsweetened apple sauce
2 tbsp vegetable oil
1 tsp almond extract
½ cup chopped walnuts (optional)

Preheat the oven to 350° F.

In a medium bowl, mix together flour, baking powder, baking soda, cinnamon and nutmeg; set aside.

In a large bowl, combine eggs, pumpkin purée, sugar, apple sauce, vegetable oil, almond extract and nuts.

Slowly add the flour mixture to the pumpkin mixture and stir only until just blended. Do not over mix.

Spoon the batter into 18 non-stick muffin cups.

Bake in oven for 25 to 30 minutes.

Makes 18 muffins

Little Helper

Measure out first five dry ingredients and place in a mixing bowl.

Pumpkin Bread

3 cups sugar
1 cup cooking oil
4 eggs
2 cups canned pumpkin
3½ cups all-purpose flour
1½ tsp salt
1 tsp cinnamon
1 tsp nutmeg
2 tsp baking soda
⅔ cup water
1 cup chopped pecans

Preheat oven to 350° F.

Place sugar and oil in mixer bowl and mix on low speed. Blend in 1 egg at a time. Add pumpkin, mixing well.

In a separate bowl, combine all remaining dry ingredients, except pecans. Add to pumpkin mixture, alternating with water, and ending with dry mixture. Fold in chopped pecans.

Pour mixture into well-greased large loaf pan. Bake in oven for 1 hour.

Makes 1 loaf

Halloween Sugar Cookies

2 ¾ cups all-purpose flour
1 tsp baking soda
½ tsp baking powder
1¼ cups softened butter or margarine
1½ cups sugar
¼ tsp salt
2 large egg yolks
1½ tsp vanilla
Egg wash (beat 1 egg white lightly with 2 tsp water)
Orange-colored decorating sugar

In a small bowl, stir together flour, baking soda and baking powder; set aside.

In a large bowl with an electric mixer, cream the butter with the sugar until the mixture is light and fluffy.

Add the salt, egg yolks and vanilla; beat the mixture until smooth.

Add the flour mixture and beat the dough until it is just combined.

Divide the dough into 4 equal parts.

Shape dough into 4 disks, wrap with plastic wrap and refrigerate for about 1 hour, or until firm.

Preheat oven to 375° F.

Roll out dough between 2 sheets of waxed paper, about ¼-inch thick for crispier cookies and ⅓-inch thick for softer cookies.

Cut out various shapes with assorted Halloween cookie cutters and place on ungreased baking sheets, about 1 inch apart.

Brush the cookies lightly with the egg wash; sprinkle them with the decorating sugar.

Bake for 7-8 minutes, or until edges just start to turn a golden color. (For softer cookies, do not allow the cookies to take on color.)

Remove from oven, let cool for one minute and then transfer to wire rack to cool completely.

Makes 2 dozen

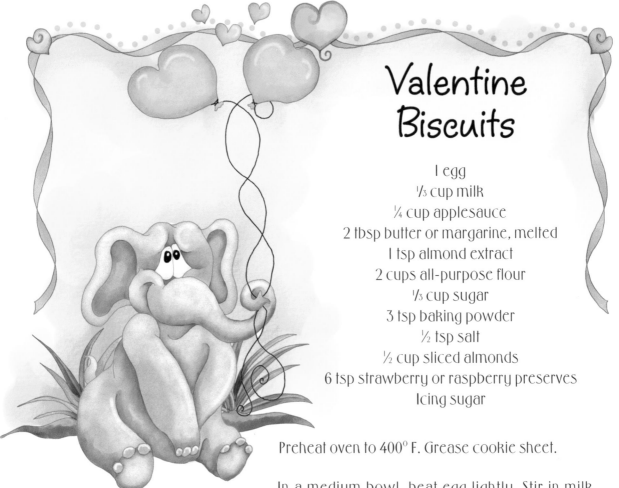

Valentine Biscuits

1 egg
⅓ cup milk
¼ cup applesauce
2 tbsp butter or margarine, melted
1 tsp almond extract
2 cups all-purpose flour
⅓ cup sugar
3 tsp baking powder
½ tsp salt
½ cup sliced almonds
6 tsp strawberry or raspberry preserves
Icing sugar

Preheat oven to 400° F. Grease cookie sheet.

In a medium bowl, beat egg lightly. Stir in milk, applesauce, butter and almond extract. Add flour, sugar, baking powder, salt and sliced almonds; mix until moistened.

Divide dough into 9 parts. Place dough pieces on cookie sheet, about 3 inches apart. Dust fingers with flour, pat dough pieces into heart shapes, about 3 inches wide and ½ inch high. Make shallow well in center of each heart. Fill each well with about ½ tsp preserves.

Bake in oven for 12 to 15 minutes, or until golden brown. Remove from cookie sheet to wire rack.

Sprinkle with icing sugar while still warm. Serve.

Makes 9 biscuits

Spoon some berry preserves in center of each heart.

Chocolate Hearts

1½ cups brown sugar
⅔ cup Crisco shortening
1 tbsp water
1 tsp vanilla
2 eggs
1½ cups all-purpose flour
⅓ cup cocoa powder
¼ tsp baking soda
½ tsp salt
2 cups miniature semi-sweet chocolate chips
½ cup white chocolate chips
Red candied cherries

Preheat oven to 375° F. Place sheets of foil on countertop for cooling cookies.

In a large bowl, combine brown sugar, shortening, water and vanilla; mix until well blended. Beat eggs into creamed mixture.

In a separate bowl, combine flour, cocoa, baking soda and salt. Stir into creamed mixture until well blended. Stir in dark chocolate chips.

Divide dough in half. Spread dough into 2 ungreased 8-inch round cake pans.

Bake one pan at a time at 375° F. for 10 to 12 minutes. Do not over bake. Cool 5 minutes in pan.

Cut with 2-inch heart-shaped cookie cutter, with point towards center, to make 12 cookies. Remove cookies to foil to cool completely.

Place white chocolate chips in a microwave-safe shallow bowl and heat in microwave on HIGH for 30 seconds; stir. Repeat until chocolate is melted. Spread melted chocolate on top of cooled hearts. Top each cookie with red candied cherry. Set aside to dry completely.

Makes 1 dozen

Irish Scones

½ cup butter
2 cups all-purpose flour
2 tsp baking powder
½ tsp salt
½ cup sugar
¾ cup raisins, dates or other dried fruit
2 eggs
½ cup plus I tbsp milk

Preheat oven to 350° F.

In a large bowl, combine butter and flour until crumbly. Add baking powder, salt, sugar and raisins; stir to mix.

In a separate bowl, whisk together I egg and ½ cup milk. Gradually stir into flour mixture until a dough forms. Work dough with hands, if necessary.

Divide dough into 12 pieces; drop onto an ungreased baking sheet.

In a small bowl, beat together remaining egg and I tbsp milk to make an egg wash. Lightly brush each scone with egg wash.

Bake in oven for 20-25 minutes, or until lightly golden.

Makes 12 scones

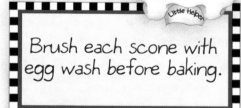

Little Helper

Brush each scone with egg wash before baking.

Shamrock Cookies

1 cup butter, softened
1½ cups powdered sugar
1 egg
2 tsp vanilla extract
1 tsp cream of tartar
¼ tsp ground nutmeg
2½ cups all-purpose flour
1 tsp baking soda

Preheat oven to 375° F. Grease cookie sheet.

In a large bowl, cream together butter and sugar until light and fluffy.

Add egg, vanilla, cream of tartar and ground nutmeg; mix well.

Combine flour and baking soda and slowly add to creamed mixture. Chill dough.

On lightly floured surface, roll out dough to ⅛-inch thickness.

Cut dough into shamrock shapes with cookie cutter.

Bake in oven for 8-10 minutes, or until lightly browned.

Cool cookies completely on wire racks before decorating with green icing.

Green Icing
10 drops green food coloring
2-3 tsp milk
½ cup powdered sugar

In a small bowl, mix drops of green food coloring with milk.

Add powdered sugar, stirring until color is evenly distributed and icing is smooth.

Makes about 2 dozen cookies

Broiled Lemon and Garlic Tiger Prawns

1½ lbs. tiger prawns,
peeled and deveined
1 cup butter
1 tsp minced garlic
1½ tbsp lemon juice
3 tbsp grated Parmesan cheese

Preheat oven on broiler setting.

With a sharp knife, remove tails from prawns, and butterfly them from the underside. Arrange prawns on broiler pan.

In a small saucepan, melt butter with garlic and lemon juice.

Pour ¼ cup butter mixture in a small bowl, and brush onto prawns.

Sprinkle Parmesan cheese over shrimp.

Place broiler pan on top rack of oven; broil prawns for 4 to 5 minutes, or until done. Serve with remaining butter mixture for dipping.

Serves 6

Note: A special starter for special occasions.

Rosemary Leg of Lamb

5-lb. leg of lamb
4 cloves garlic, sliced
Salt to taste
Ground black pepper to taste
Fresh rosemary sprigs
½ cup Dijon mustard
1 tbsp all-purpose flour

Preheat oven to 325° F.

Cut slits in the top of the leg of lamb every 3-4 inches, deep enough to push slices of garlic into the meat. Season generously with salt and pepper all over the top of lamb.

Place several sprigs of fresh rosemary under and on top of the lamb. Smear the mustard all over the lamb and sprinkle it with a fine coating of flour.

Roast, uncovered, until medium-well, or desired doneness (about 20 minutes per pound for a pink roast). Use the pan drippings to make a gravy by adding a little flour and water.

Serves 12

Easter Bunny Cake

1 box of your favorite cake mix (water, eggs and oil as needed)
2 cups white or butter cream frosting
3 cups flaked coconut
Red food coloring

Green food coloring
Assorted candies for garnish
(eg. jellybeans, gumdrops, string licorice, red Twizzlers candy, mini chocolate chips)

Bake two 9-inch cake rounds according to package directions; cool to room temperature.

Turn one cake layer out onto a large rectangular platter; this will be the bunny's face (head). The second layer will become the bunny's ears and bowtie: cut two sides of the round cake layer into bunny ears in a () shape, leaving a bowtie shape in the middle. Place the two bunny ears at the top of the bunny's head and place the bowtie at the bottom. Frost the cake with white or butter cream frosting, covering all the sides.

Place 1 cup coconut into a zip-lock plastic bag; add a few drops of red food coloring; shake. Sprinkle the pink coconut all over the top and sides of the bowtie and on the middle of the bunny ears. Cover the rest of the bunny with 1 cup of white coconut.
Repeat steps above to make some green coconut for the "grass" around the cake. Sprinkle the green coconut all around the platter.

Decorate the face with candies. Use gumdrops for eyes and nose, thin licorice strips for the whiskers, a red Twizzlers candy for the mouth, chocolate chips for the outlines of ears and bowtie. Use jelly beans to decorate the bowtie.
Sprinkle the leftover jelly beans all around the bunny, and throughout the green coconut grass.

Serves 16

Chocolate Animals

3 cups semi-sweet chocolate chips
14-oz can sweetened condensed milk
   (not evaporated)
Dash salt
1 cup chopped walnuts (optional)
1½ tsp vanilla

Line a 13x9x2-inch pan with foil, extending
foil over edges of pan; set aside.

In a saucepan, over low heat, melt chips
with milk and salt. Remove from heat; stir
in walnuts and vanilla.

Spread mixture evenly into prepared pan. Refrigerate 2 hours, or until firm.

Use foil to lift fudge out of pan. Place on a cutting board.

Peel off foil; cut into desired shapes with animal-shaped cookie cutters.
Store, tightly covered, in a cool dry place.

Makes about 2 lbs. of fudge

Party Nut Balls

1 cup whole-wheat bread crumbs
¾ cup grated mozzarella cheese
½ cup finely chopped pecans
¼ cup finely chopped almonds
1 egg, beaten
⅓ cup minced shallots (or onions)
1 clove garlic, minced
1 tsp Tamari soy sauce
½ tsp ground sage
¼ tsp cinnamon
½ tsp pepper

Preheat oven to 350° F.

In a large bowl, combine all ingredients and stir well to blend.

Using clean hands, form the mixture into about 24 balls (the size of a walnut in its shell). Place the balls on a baking sheet coated with cooking spray.

Bake until lightly browned, about 15 minutes, turning about halfway through.

Nut balls can be served with tomato sauce, peanut sauce, or Caesar dressing for dipping.

Serves 4-6

Party Pickle Rolls

8-oz. pkg. cream cheese
10 (6-inch) flour tortillas
1 lb. sliced ham
32-oz. jar dill pickles

Spread cream cheese on one side of a tortilla.

Place a slice or two of ham over this.

Spread another layer of cream cheese over the ham.

Roll a pickle up in the tortilla and slice the roll into finger food-sized pieces.

Refrigerate the rolls if you aren't serving them immediately.

Serves 15-20

Sweet Potato Balls

4 large cooked and mashed
   sweet potatoes
3 tsp butter
1 tsp salt
⅛ tsp pepper
Pinch of cinnamon and nutmeg
2-3 tbsp brown sugar
Crushed cornflakes or honey-
   nut flakes

Preheat oven to 350° F.
In a large bowl, mix together sweet potatoes, butter, salt, pepper, cinnamon, nutmeg and brown sugar until well combined. Shape small scoops of potato mixture into balls. Roll balls in crushed flakes. Bake in oven for 20 minutes.

Makes about 14 medium-size balls

Swedish Meatballs

½ cup fine dry bread crumbs
3 tbsp warm milk
1 lb. ground beef or veal, or a combination
1 cup cream, divided
1 egg
Salt and pepper
1½ cups beef broth
2 tbsp flour
2 tbsp water
1 egg yolk

In a large bowl, soften bread crumbs with milk; add meat. Stir in ½ cup cream and mix. Add egg, salt and pepper; stir well. Roll mixture into balls.
In a saucepan, heat broth, add meatballs and cook gently for 15 minutes. With a slotted spoon, transfer meatballs to a serving bowl; set aside. Reserve broth.
Just before serving, mix flour with water and add to broth. Bring to a boil and cook 3 minutes. Add remaining ½ cup cream blended with the egg yolk. Season to taste and pour over meatballs.

Serves 8

Red, White and Blue Shortcake

18-oz. pkg. angel food cake mix
8-oz. container frozen whipped topping, thawed
1 pint blueberries, rinsed and drained
2 pints fresh strawberries, rinsed and sliced

Preheat oven to 350° F.
Prepare cake according to package directions and bake in a 9x13-inch pan.
Cool completely.

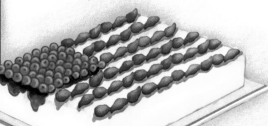

Frost cake with whipped topping.
Arrange blueberries in a square in the upper left corner of cake as "stars".
Arrange sliced strawberries as "stripes" to make an American "flag". Chill until serving time.

Variation: To decorate cake as a Canadian flag, arrange 2 rows of strawberry halves on each side of frosted cake to make wide stripes. Then make shape of maple leaf in the center, using more strawberry halves.

Serves 18

Chill until serving.

Fiesta Jelly Mold

3-oz. pkg. strawberry-flavored
gelatin (or any red flavor)
1¾ cups boiling water
½ cup cold water
1½ cups sliced strawberries
3-oz. pkg. lemon-flavored gelatin
1 pint vanilla ice cream, softened

In a bowl, mix the red gelatin with 1 cup of the boiling water, stirring for at least 2 minutes until completely dissolved. Stir in the cold water.

Place bowl of red gelatin in larger bowl of ice and water. Stir until thickened, about 8 minutes.

Wash, cut and slice strawberries. Stir strawberries into thickened gelatin. Pour mixture into a 9x5-inch loaf pan. Refrigerate 7 minutes.

Meanwhile, in a medium bowl, mix remaining ¾ cup boiling water with lemon gelatin, stirring for at least 2 minutes until completely dissolved.

Stir in ice cream until melted and smooth. Spoon this mixture over red gelatin in pan. Refrigerate 4 hours, or overnight until firm. Unmold and garnish with fruit slices, or as desired.
Store leftover gelatin mold in refrigerator.

Serves 12

When my oldest son had just started high school and my younger one was in middle school, we moved across the country. Up until then we had always lived in a hot, tropical climate. Our move took us into a four-season region. That first winter, we all got to enjoy many new experiences. With warnings of a big snow storm on the way, my sons had their fingers crossed as they watched the names of school cancellations scroll across the TV screen, happily resulting in a "Snow Day". It was on this first snow day in our new home that I discovered how wonderful a hot soup can be.

Our new yard had a fair-size hill that was perfect for sledding. Since we had never done this activity before, we were quite excited. We lined up our newly-bought saucer-style sleds and prepared to head down. Blasting off from the top of the hill, we had no idea exactly how far we would travel or where we would end up. To our surprise, the "ride" took us down our hill, under a row of low-branched trees and all the way to a neighboring house before we were able to stop. After we had figured out how to "steer" our sleds, we spent many hours that first snow day enjoying our winter wonderland.

By the end of the day we were cold and famished. We had not realized how long we had been sledding and how very cold we were. I had come into the house earlier that day and started a pot of meatball soup. Needless to say, everyone had worked up quite an appetite. The soup was ready and waiting. That was the perfect end to our first of many snow days.

Winter Warm-ups

Cream of Broccoli Soup

1 cup water
1½ cups chopped potatoes
1½ cups chopped broccoli
2 tbsp butter
1 onion, minced
2 cups chicken broth
1 tsp celery salt
Salt and pepper to taste
½ cup heavy cream

In a saucepan, bring water to a boil. Add the chopped potatoes; 5 minutes later, add the chopped broccoli. Simmer for 5 minutes; set aside. Do not drain.

In a clean saucepan or pot, melt the butter. Brown minced onion in melted butter until it becomes translucent.

Mix in potatoes and broccoli, along with cooking water. Pour in chicken broth; cook for 10 minutes.

Pour mixture into a blender; mix until smooth and well blended. Pour mixture back into pot.

Sprinkle with celery salt, salt and pepper; reheat.

Pour in cream, stirring constantly until hot. Do not let boil. Serve immediately.

Serves 4

Cheesy Cauliflower Soup

4 cups water
1 large potato, peeled and diced
1 large cauliflower, broken into florets
1 medium carrot
2 cups (packed) grated low-fat
   Cheddar cheese

1 tbsp vegetable oil
½ cup minced onions
3 medium cloves garlic, peeled
1 tsp salt
¾ cup light cream
1 tsp nutmeg

In a large soup pot, add water, potato, cauliflower and carrot. Bring to a boil, and then simmer on low heat until all the vegetables are very tender, about 20 minutes.

Purée in a blender (in batches, filling blender only ⅔ full).

Transfer puréed soup back into soup pot. Add cheese and stir until well blended.

In a frying pan, heat oil; sauté onions, garlic and salt until onions are soft and slightly browned.

Stir onion mixture into soup. Return soup to stove top. Add cream, stirring until heated through, 3-5 minutes. Sprinkle with nutmeg.

Serves 6-8

Meatball Soup

1 tbsp butter
1 cup chopped onion
1 (10 ¾ oz.) can condensed tomato soup
1 (10 ½ oz.) can condensed chicken
noodle soup
½ cup water
1 lb. ground beef or veal
1 egg
⅛ cup milk
2 slices bread

Melt butter in a large saucepan over medium heat. Sauté onion until tender.

Stir in the tomato soup, chicken noodle soup and the water; bring to a boil. Reduce heat to medium low and let simmer.

Meanwhile, combine the ground beef, egg and milk in a bowl. Break the bread into very small pieces and add to the bowl. Mix together well.

Shape the meat mixture into small meatballs and drop them into the soup mixture.

Continue to simmer, uncovered, for 20 to 30 minutes. Stir occasionally.

Serves 6

Kids love to make meatballs. Be sure they wash their hands well before and after.

Patty's Pumpkin Patch Soup

1 tbsp olive oil
1 cup chopped onion
1 tsp ground ginger
½ tsp curry powder
¼ tsp cumin
¼ tsp nutmeg
2 garlic cloves, minced
2 cups peeled, cubed sweet potatoes
2 cups low-sodium chicken broth
1½ cups water
14-oz. can pumpkin
1 cup milk
3 tbsp light sour cream

Heat olive oil in a large soup pot over medium heat. Add the onion and sauté for 3 minutes. Add the ginger, curry, cumin, nutmeg and garlic; cook for 1 minute.

Stir in the sweet potatoes, chicken broth, water and pumpkin; bring to a boil. Reduce heat and simmer for 15 to 20 minutes or until the sweet potato is soft, stirring occasionally. Stir in the milk until heated through. Do not let boil.

Carefully ladle half of the soup (about 3 cups) into a 5-cup blender. Blend on purée setting until smooth. Repeat with rest of soup. Ladle soup into bowls and top each with ½ tbsp sour cream.

Soup can be made ahead of time and refrigerated up to 4 days. Reheat in a saucepan over medium heat or microwave on high for 1-2 minutes.

Makes 6 (1-cup) servings

Chicken and Dumpling Soup

2½- 3 lb. fryer chicken, cut up
6 cups cold water
3 chicken bouillon cubes
6 peppercorns
3 whole cloves
10 ¾-oz. can chicken broth
1 can cream of chicken soup
1 cup diced potatoes
1 cup chopped celery
¼ cup chopped onion
1½ cups chopped carrots
1 cup fresh or frozen peas
1 bay leaf
Salt and pepper to taste

Dumplings

2 cups all-purpose flour
1 tsp salt
4 tsp baking powder
1 egg, well beaten
2 tbsp melted butter
⅔ cup milk

Place chicken in large pot with water, bouillon cubes, peppercorns and cloves; bring to a boil. Simmer for 1½ hours, or until chicken is tender.

Take out chicken; remove meat from bones, discarding skin and bones. Cut chicken into pieces. Skim broth and strain out spices. Return chicken meat to broth. Add all remaining soup ingredients, and let simmer for 1½ to 2 hours.

About 30 minutes before serving, make dumplings by sifting together flour, salt and baking powder. Combine egg, melted butter and milk and add to flour mixture, stirring quickly just until smooth.

Drop by spoonfuls into simmering soup. Cover tightly and let simmer 18 to 20 minutes more until done.

Serves 12

Japanese Chicken Noodle Soup

10 ½-oz. pkg. Japanese Udon noodles
1 large carrot, cut in three
1 stalk celery, cut in three
1 large onion, quartered
1 sprig fresh cilantro, leaves and stem
2 whole chicken breasts
2 chicken thighs
16 cups water
Salt and pepper to taste

Prepare Udon noodles by boiling about 6 cups of water, or enough to cover noodles in a large pot. Slowly add Udon noodles to the boiling water. Bring to a boil again and stir the noodles. Add 1 cup cold water and bring to a boil again.

Turn down the heat and cook noodles until tender (the cooking time differs, depending on the kind of Udon). Drain noodles in a strainer and cool them under running cold water. Cover and set aside.

In a food processor or blender, finely chop the vegetables and cilantro.

In a large soup pot, place the chicken in water with the finely chopped vegetables, cilantro, salt and pepper. Bring to a boil, then reduce heat and simmer, covered, for 1-2 hours, or until chicken is cooked. Remove chicken.

The cooked chicken can be chopped and added to the soup for a heartier meal, or used to make your favorite chicken salad recipe.

Add cooked Udon noodles to soup and heat for another 5-7 minutes before serving.

Serves 6-8

Tortilla Soup

1 tbsp olive oil
1 large onion, chopped
2 cloves garlic, minced
1 tbsp cumin
¼ tsp ground coriander
1 tbsp chili powder
1 tbsp oregano
¼ tsp cayenne pepper
1¼ cups coarsely chopped tortilla chips
1 cup tomato juice
1 cup chicken stock
½ cup grated Cheddar cheese
½ cup light sour cream

In a large soup pot, heat olive oil. Sauté onion and garlic with the spices for 1-2 minutes.

Stir in 1 cup tortilla chips; add tomato juice and chicken stock and then bring to a boil.

Reduce heat and simmer for 30 minutes.

Ladle into 4 soup bowls.

Garnish with remaining tortilla chips, Cheddar cheese and sour cream.

Serves 4

Hurry-Up Fill-Me-Up Burritos

½ cup cooked rice
½ cup kidney beans, rinsed
½ cup kernel corn
¾ cup prepared salsa
10 small (6-inch) flour or corn tortillas, warmed
1¼ cups shredded mozzarella cheese
½ cup light sour cream

In a non-stick pan, combine rice, beans, corn and salsa; stir over medium heat until warmed through, about 3-4 minutes.

Divide mixture evenly amongst the warmed tortillas. Sprinkle with cheese. Roll up tortillas. Dip in sour cream and enjoy!

Tip: These can also be prepared in the microwave: combine rice, beans, corn and salsa in a medium bowl. Divide mixture amongst tortillas; sprinkle with cheese and roll up. Microwave on HIGH for 30-40 seconds, or until heated through.

Makes 10 burritos

Little Helper

Sprinkle cheese over filled tortillas and roll up tightly.

Taco Salad

3 lbs. ground beef
1 cup chopped onions
1 green pepper, chopped
1 can Ro*Tel tomatoes
3 pkg. taco mix
Lettuce
Tortilla chips, crushed
2 lbs. Velveeta cheese

In a large frying pan or skillet, brown meat with onions. Stir in green pepper, tomatoes and taco mix. Cook for 5 minutes.

Place lettuce and crushed chips on serving platter. Spoon meat mixture over.

In a saucepan, melt cheese and drizzle over salad. Serve immediately.

Serves 6

Onion Ring-a-dings

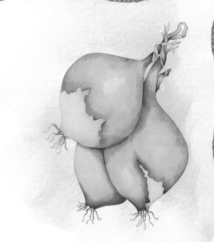

3 large yellow onions
2 eggs, separated
1½ cups beer, room temperature
⅓ cup melted butter
2 cups all-purpose flour
6 cups vegetable oil for deep frying
¼ cup flour for coating
Salt

Peel onions and slice about ¼-inch thick; separate into rings.

In a large bowl, beat egg yolks until light colored; stir in beer and butter. Stir in 2 cups flour; let stand 30 minutes. Beat egg whites until stiff peaks form; fold into batter.

Heat oil to 375° F.

Dredge onion rings in flour to coat; shake off excess flour. Dip onion rings in batter; let excess batter drip off. Drop several rings at a time into hot oil and fry until golden.

Drain on paper towels. Sprinkle with salt and serve.

Serves 6

Carefully separate onion slices into rings.

Soft Gingerbread

1 cup sorghum molasses
½ cup butter
1½ tsp baking soda
½ cup sour milk
2 eggs, beaten well
2 cups all-purpose flour
2 tsp ginger
½ tsp salt

Preheat oven to 350° F.
In a saucepan, heat molasses and butter over medium heat and bring to a boil.
Remove from heat and add baking soda. Beat well and let cool.
Stir in milk and eggs.
Sift together the remaining dry ingredients and add to molasses, mixing well.
Pour into a well-greased cake pan and bake for 40 minutes.
Serve warm with butter or whipped cream.

Serves 8

Apple-Squash Crisp

1 medium butternut squash
1 medium apple
¼ cup packed brown sugar
¼ cup butter or margarine, softened

1½ tsp all-purpose flour
½ tsp salt
¼ tsp cinnamon

Preheat oven to 350° F.
Peel, seed and cut squash into ½-inch slices. Peel apple and cut into thin slices.
Arrange squash slices in an 8-inch square baking pan coated with vegetable
cooking spray. Place apple slices over squash.
In a small bowl, combine rest of ingredients until well blended. Drop by spoonfuls
over apple-squash mixture.
Cover and bake for 30 minutes. Let stand 5 minutes before serving.

Serves 4

Spiced Tea

3 quarts water
1 tsp whole cloves
3 cinnamon sticks
6 regular tea bags
1½ cups sugar

2 cups water
Juice of 3 oranges
Juice of 3 lemons
Orange slices

In a large stainless steel Dutch oven, combine 3 quarts of water, cloves and cinnamon sticks; bring to a boil.

Remove from heat and add tea bags; cover and steep 15 minutes. Discard tea bags, cloves and cinnamon sticks. Set tea aside.

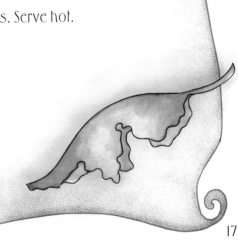

In a small stainless steel saucepan; combine the sugar, 2 cups of water and juices; bring to a boil, stirring frequently until sugar dissolves.

Combine tea mixture and juice mixture, stirring until well blended.

Pour into serving cups and garnish with orange slices. Serve hot.

Makes about 3 ½ quarts

Kids love pajama parties! We used to call them "slumber" parties. My mom would always comment that there was never much "slumbering" going on. My kids called them "sleepovers". Whatever the name, if you plan to host one, brace yourself for a houseful of very excited kids bent on non-stop fun, and, don't plan on getting any sleep yourself.

A pajama party "must" is to have plenty of food available for your boisterous houseguests. And you too are going to need nourishment to help get you through the event. Your kids will definitely enjoy helping you prepare their pajama party menu. This chapter will give you several great ideas to help make your kids' overnight party a success.

Pajama Party

Thick and Chunky Salsa

3 medium tomatoes, seeded and
chopped (2 ¼ cups)
1 small green bell pepper, chopped (½ cup)
3 cloves garlic, finely chopped
½ cup sliced green onions
2 tbsp chopped fresh cilantro, or parsley
2 tbsp lime juice
¼ tsp salt

Mix together all ingredients in a small plastic bowl, with lid.
Cover and refrigerate at least 1 hour to blend flavors.

Makes about 3 cups

Quick Guacamole and Chips

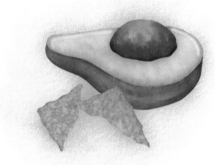

1 large, ripe avocado, mashed
¼ cup thick-and-chunky salsa (store bought or homemade)
½ tbsp lime juice
40-50 tortilla chips (store bought or homemade)

Mix avocado, salsa and lime juice together in a small bowl; cover with a lid and
refrigerate.

Serve ¼ cup of guacamole with 10-12 tortilla chips per serving.

Makes about 1 cup of dip (Serves 4)

Homemade Baked Tortilla Chips

10 (7-inch) flour tortillas
1 tbsp sesame (or vegetable) oil
2 tbsp lime juice
1 tsp chili powder
½ tsp salt

Preheat oven to 350° F.

Cut each tortilla into 8 pie-shaped wedge sections. Arrange tortilla wedges in a single layer on a cookie sheet.

In a mister (or clean spray bottle), combine oil and lime juice. Shake to mix well and spray each tortilla wedge until slightly moist.

In a small bowl, combine chili powder and salt. Sprinkle evenly on tortilla wedges. Bake for about 15 minutes (rotate pan at 7-minute mark), or until chips are crisp, but not too brown.

Store in an air-tight container to preserve freshness.

Makes 80 tortilla chips

Arrange tortilla wedges on a cookie sheet and spray to moisten.

Late-Night Wraps

6 (10-inch) flour tortillas
4-oz. pkg. cream cheese
½ head lettuce
3-oz. pkg. sliced deli-style turkey
1 cup shredded carrots
1 cup diced tomatoes

Spread cream cheese evenly over tortillas. Top with lettuce leaves. Lay turkey slices on top.
Sprinkle carrots and tomatoes over turkey slices.
Roll tortillas into wraps. Cut the wraps into bite-sized pieces. Secure with toothpicks.

Serves 6

Zesty Zucchini Sticks

4 medium zucchini
¼ cup cornmeal
¼ cup all-purpose flour
¼ cup grated Parmesan cheese

½ to ¾ tsp garlic salt
¼ tsp paprika
¼ tsp oregano
1 egg, beaten

Preheat oven to 350° F.
Slice each zucchini lengthwise to make 8 spears.
In a large bowl, combine cornmeal, flour, cheese, garlic salt, paprika and oregano.
Dip zucchini spears into the beaten egg, and then dredge in cornmeal mixture.
Place on baking sheet, coated with vegetable cooking spray.
Bake at 350° F for 15 minutes.

Serves 4-6

Pizza Cookies

1 cup margarine
1 cup peanut butter
1 cup sugar
1 cup packed brown sugar
2 eggs
1¼ cups all-purpose flour
1 tsp baking soda
½ tsp salt
2¼ cups quick oats, uncooked
1 cup plain M & M candies

Preheat oven to 325° F.

In a large mixer bowl, beat together margarine, peanut butter, sugar and brown sugar until light and fluffy.

Beat in eggs; add flour, baking soda and salt. Mix well. Stir in oats and ⅓ cup of candies.

To make 2 pizza-size cookies, place half the dough onto each of 2 foil-lined and greased 12-13-inch pizza pans.

Spread dough to within 1 inch of edge of pan. Garnish each cookie with ⅓ cup candies.

Bake in oven until done, about 15 minutes.

Cut like pizza slices to serve.

Makes 2 pizzas

Best-Ever Brownies

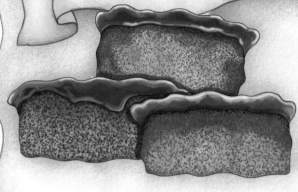

½ cup melted butter or margarine
1 cup sugar
1 tsp vanilla extract
2 large eggs
½ cup all-purpose flour
⅓ cup cocoa
¼ tsp baking powder
¼ tsp salt
½ cup chopped nuts (optional)

Preheat oven to 350° F.
Grease a 9-inch square baking pan.

In a bowl, mix together butter, sugar and vanilla; add eggs and beat well with spoon.

In a separate bowl, mix together flour, cocoa, baking powder and salt; gradually add to egg mixture, beating until well blended. Stir in nuts, if desired.

Spread batter evenly into prepared pan. Bake 20 to 25 minutes, or until brownies begin to pull away from sides of pan. Cool completely in pan on wire rack.

Creamy Brownie Frosting

3 tbsp softened butter or margarine
3 tbsp cocoa
1 tbsp light corn syrup
½ tsp vanilla extract
1 cup icing sugar
1 to 2 tbsp milk

In a bowl, beat butter, cocoa, corn syrup and vanilla until well blended.
Add sugar and milk; beat to smooth consistency.
Spread over brownies. Cut into squares.

Makes 16 brownies

Bear Paws

1 cup butter or margarine, softened
⅔ cup sugar
½ cup chocolate syrup
2 large eggs
1 tsp vanilla extract
¼ cup milk
2 cups all-purpose flour
2 tsp baking powder
1 tsp salt
Peanut halves or cashew nuts

In a large mixing bowl, cream butter and sugar until light and fluffy. Stir in chocolate syrup. Add eggs, beating well. Blend in vanilla and milk.

Combine flour, baking powder and salt. Add to chocolate mixture, blending well. Cover dough and chill 1 hour.

Preheat oven to 350° F.

Drop heaping teaspoonfuls of dough, 2 inches apart, onto greased baking sheets. Press 4 peanut halves into each cookie to resemble paws.

Bake 8 to 10 minutes, or until centers spring back when lightly touched. Remove from baking sheets and transfer to wire racks; let cool completely.

Makes 3 dozen

Little Helper

Press nuts into cookies
to look like paws.

Midnight Blue Muffins

1¼ cups all-purpose flour
1 tsp baking soda
2 tsp cream of tartar
¼ cup sugar
½ tsp salt

1 egg, beaten
½ cup milk
⅓ cup shortening, melted
1 cup blueberries, drained

Preheat oven to 400° F.
In a large bowl, sift together the dry ingredients.
Make a well in the middle and add egg, milk and melted shortening; mix well.
Carefully fold in the blueberries. Spoon into greased muffin tins.
Bake in oven for 18-20 minutes.

Makes 1 dozen muffins

Easy Caramel Popcorn

2 cups brown sugar, firmly packed
1 cup butter or margarine
½ cup light corn syrup
2 tsp salt
1 tsp baking soda
1 cup peanuts or pecans
7½ quarts of popped popcorn

Preheat oven to 200° F.
In a saucepan, combine brown sugar, butter, corn syrup and salt. Bring to a boil; boil 5 minutes. Beat in baking soda vigorously. Stir in nuts.
Place popcorn in a large shallow pan. Pour sugar mixture over popcorn; stir.
Bake in oven for 1 hour, stirring every 15 minutes.

Makes 7 quarts

Sweet Dreams Dip

8 oz. light cream cheese, softened
¼ cup packed brown sugar
¾ cup canned pumpkin
1 tsp ground cinnamon
2 tsp maple syrup
½ winter squash, any kind
4 apples cut into wedges (or other favorite fruit)

Place all ingredients (except winter squash and apples) in a bowl and beat with a mixer at medium speed until mixed well. Cover and chill for 30 minutes. Clean out seeds and insides from winter squash with a large spoon. Once chilled, spoon dip into squash "bowl". Serve with apple slices or other favorite fruit.

Serves 4-6

Cracker Candy

Plain soda crackers
1 cup brown sugar
2 sticks butter
12-oz. pkg. chocolate chips

Preheat oven to 400° F.
Line a 13x9x2-inch pan with foil. Arrange crackers in single layer on foil.
In a medium saucepan, bring the brown sugar and butter to a boil; boil for 3 minutes. Pour liquid over crackers and bake in oven for 7-8 minutes.
Remove from oven and sprinkle chocolate chips over the crackers. As chips melt, spread with the back of a large spoon.
Cool until hardened. Break or cut into pieces.

Serves 4-6

Tutti-Fruitti Drops

1 cup softened butter or margarine
2 cups packed brown sugar
2 eggs
½ cup buttermilk
3½ cups all-purpose flour
1 tsp baking soda
1 tsp salt
1 ½ cups chopped walnuts
2 cups candied cherries, halved
2 cups dates, pitted and chopped

In a large bowl, cream together butter and brown sugar. Beat in eggs and buttermilk. Add flour, baking soda and salt. Once well combined, stir in chopped nuts, candied cherries and chopped dates. Cover and refrigerate dough for at least 1 hour.

Preheat oven to 400° F.

Drop small spoonfuls of chilled dough onto lightly greased baking sheet.

Bake for 8 to 10 minutes.

Makes 8 dozen

Drop spoonfuls of dough onto baking sheet.

Dream Balls

1 stick margarine
1 cup sugar
8-oz. pkg. chopped dates
1 egg
1 cup Rice Krispies cereal
¾ cup chopped pecans
Shredded coconut

In a saucepan, combine margarine, sugar, dates and egg.

Cook on low heat for about 10 minutes, being careful not to let mixture burn; cool.
Stir in Rice Krispies and pecans.

Shape mixture into balls; roll in coconut. Place on waxed paper until cooled.

Makes approximately 20 balls

Bedtime Shake

½ banana
½ cup fresh or frozen berries
½ cup milk or vanilla-flavored soy milk
½ cup low-fat vanilla or fruit-flavored yogurt

In a blender, combine all ingredients and blend until smooth.
Pour into your favorite cup and enjoy!
If shake is too thick, add extra milk or soy milk until desired consistency is reached.

Serves 1

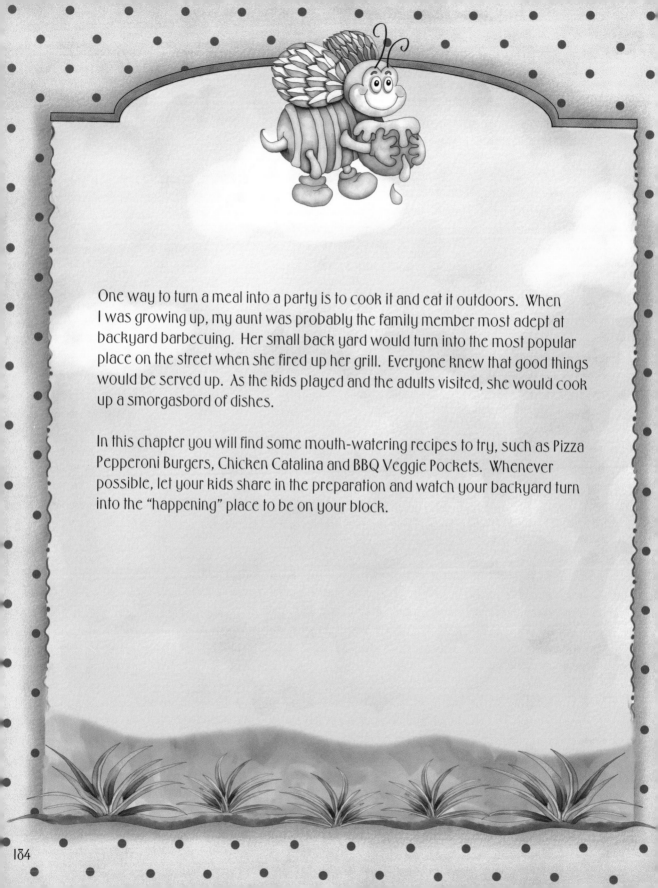

One way to turn a meal into a party is to cook it and eat it outdoors. When I was growing up, my aunt was probably the family member most adept at backyard barbecuing. Her small back yard would turn into the most popular place on the street when she fired up her grill. Everyone knew that good things would be served up. As the kids played and the adults visited, she would cook up a smorgasbord of dishes.

In this chapter you will find some mouth-watering recipes to try, such as Pizza Pepperoni Burgers, Chicken Catalina and BBQ Veggie Pockets. Whenever possible, let your kids share in the preparation and watch your backyard turn into the "happening" place to be on your block.

Backyard BBQ

Pizza Pepperoni Burgers

1 lb. lean ground beef
¼ lb. pepperoni sausage, minced
¼ cup Italian-seasoned bread crumbs
1 clove garlic, minced
½ cup pizza sauce
6 onion hamburger buns
1 cup grated mozzarella cheese

Preheat grill at high heat.

In a bowl, mix together ground beef, pepperoni, bread crumbs, garlic and pizza sauce. Form into burger patties.

Oil the grill grate. Place burger patties on the grill and cook 5 minutes on each side, or until well done.

Toast onion buns.

To assemble hamburgers, place one patty on each bun bottom, sprinkle grated mozzarella cheese on top of patty and cover with bun top.

Serves 6

Gobble-Gobble Burgers

Sauce
½ cup ketchup
1 tbsp Worcestershire sauce
¼ tsp black pepper

Burgers
1 lb. ground turkey
⅓ cup quick-cooking oats
4 whole-wheat hamburger buns

Preheat barbecue or broiler.

Sauce: In a small bowl, combine ketchup, Worcestershire sauce and pepper; set aside.

Burgers: In a large bowl, combine turkey and oats. Add half the sauce; mix thoroughly. Form into 4 large patties.

Barbecue on greased grill or broil 6 inches (15 cm) from heat for 5 to 7 minutes per side.

Brush with remaining sauce after burgers have been turned.

Insert patties in buns, garnish with your favorite toppings and enjoy.

Serves 4

Little Helper

Form turkey meat mixture into patties.

Honey-Barbecue Sausage Hoagies

2 lbs. Italian sausage, cut into 8-10 slices
1 large red bell pepper, cut into large chunks
1 large red onion, cut into chunks
1½ cups honey-mustard barbecue sauce
8 hoagie rolls, split lengthwise
½ lb. sliced Provolone cheese

Place sausage, red bell pepper, red onion and honey-mustard barbecue sauce in a large bowl. Cover and allow to marinate in refrigerator for at least 1 hour.

Preheat grill to high heat and oil lightly.

Place sausage and vegetable mixture on grill and baste with honey-mustard marinade; discard remaining marinade.

Grill for 8-10 minutes, turning occasionally.

Place cooked sausage and vegetables on hoagie rolls. Top with one slice Provolone cheese.

Serves 8

Blueberry Barbecue Sauce

1 cup fresh blueberries
1½ cups ketchup
⅛ cup brown sugar
¼ tsp mustard powder
2 tbsp balsamic vinegar

In a food processor, purée blueberries.
In a medium bowl, mix together puréed blueberries, ketchup, brown sugar,
mustard powder and balsamic vinegar until well blended.
Use to baste pork, beef, or chicken while grilling.

Makes 2 cups

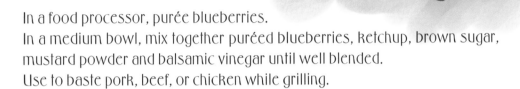

Easy Hot Dog Relish

1 cup chopped onion
½ cup chopped green bell pepper
½ cup chopped dill pickles
¼ cup chopped pimento pepper
¼ cup chopped celery

¼ cup chopped sweet pickles
1 cup brown or yellow mustard
1 cup ketchup
¼ cup prepared horseradish
2 tsp Worcestershire sauce

In a large bowl, mix together all ingredients.
Place mixture in a covered container.
May be refrigerated for up to 5 days.

Makes about 4 cups

Barbecued Chicken Thighs

½ cup soy sauce
2 tbsp sugar
1 tbsp brown sugar
1 tbsp white wine vinegar
1 tsp dry mustard
½ tsp garlic powder
¼ tsp onion powder
½ tbsp pepper
12 chicken thighs with skin
Vegetable oil or non-stick cooking spray

In a large bowl, combine soy sauce, both sugars, vinegar and spices; stir well to completely dissolve sugar.

Add chicken thighs and coat well. Cover, refrigerate, and let marinate for at least 4 hours or overnight.

Lightly brush a grill rack with vegetable oil or spray with non-stick cooking spray.

Grill chicken, uncovered, on charcoal grill with low-heat coals, or on gas grill at medium-high. Cook about 5 minutes, or until surfaces begin to brown, then turn. Keep turning thighs every 5 minutes until cooked through.

Serves 6

Chicken Catalina

4-5 boneless chicken breasts
8-oz. bottle Catalina dressing

In a large bowl, marinate chicken breasts in Catalina dressing for 20 minutes.
Cook on barbecue grill, turning often, until meat is no longer pink.

Serves 4-5

Note: Serve with corn-on-the-cob and salad.

Chicken Kebabs

4 skinless, boneless chicken breast halves, cubed
1 large green bell pepper, cut into 2-inch pieces
1 onion, cut into wedges
1 large red bell pepper, cut into 2-inch pieces
1 cup barbecue sauce
Skewers

Preheat grill for high heat.
Thread skewers, in alternating order, with
chicken, green bell pepper, onion, and red bell
pepper pieces.
Lightly oil the grill grate. Place kebabs on the
prepared grill, and brush with barbecue sauce.
Cook, turning and brushing with barbecue sauce
frequently, for 15 minutes, or until chicken juices
run clear.

Serves 4

Pork Kebabs

8 (8-inch) wooden skewers
1 lb. lean pork loin or tenderloin, cubed
1½ cups cubed fresh pineapple
1 red bell pepper, cut into chunks
1 green bell pepper, cut into chunks
1 sweet onion, cut into chunks

1 pint cherry tomatoes
¼ cup sodium-reduced soy sauce
2 tbsp lemon juice
2 tbsp honey or brown sugar
1 tsp vegetable oil
½ tsp minced ginger root

Soak wooden skewers in warm water for 30 minutes to prevent them from burning on the barbecue.

Prepare pork and vegetables, using a separate knife and cutting surface.

In a medium bowl, combine soy sauce, lemon juice, honey, oil and ginger. Add pork cubes, tossing to coat. Cover and marinate for at least 30 minutes, or overnight in refrigerator.

Thread skewers, alternating pieces of pork, pineapple, red pepper, green pepper, onion, and tomatoes. Brush kebabs with marinade; discard any leftover marinade.

Preheat barbecue or broiler.

Barbecue kebabs over medium-high heat, turning once, for 10 to 12 minutes, or until pork is just slightly pink in the center.

If desired, grill under broiler, turning once, for 8 to 10 minutes, or until cooked through.

Serves 4

Barbecued Pork Ribs

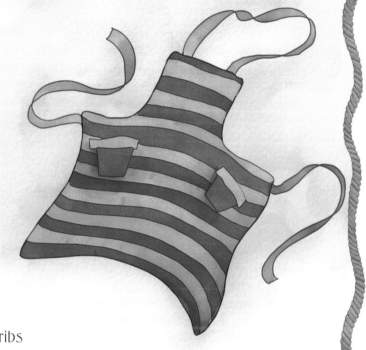

2 onions, chopped
2 cups ketchup
¼ cup cider vinegar
¼ cup lemon juice
2 tbsp prepared mustard
¼ cup brown sugar
2 tsp salt
1 tsp ground black pepper
¼ cup orange juice
1 tsp orange marmalade
1 tsp Tabasco sauce
3 lbs. pork spare ribs or back ribs

In a medium bowl, combine onions, ketchup, vinegar, lemon juice, mustard, brown sugar, salt, ground black pepper, orange juice, marmalade and Tabasco sauce.

Place ribs, bone-sides down, on greased grill over low heat.

Grill, uncovered, 30 minutes on each side. Then, brush with barbecue sauce mixture.

Grill an additional 30 minutes or until cooked through, turning and brushing with barbecue sauce mixture every 10 minutes. Total cooking time should be approx. 90 minutes.

Serves 6

Easy Lemon-Marinated Lamb Chops

3 tbsp lemon juice
½ tsp salt
3 tbsp olive oil
1 tbsp finely chopped mint leaves
½ tsp ground pepper
8 loin lamb chops

In a shallow dish, combine all ingredients and pour over lamb chops.

Cover dish and allow to marinate for at least one hour at room temperature, turning chops every 15 minutes.

Barbecue on high 3 minutes per side, or until desired doneness.

Serves 4-8

Barbecued Peaches 'n Cream

6 ears of "peaches and cream" corn
6 tbsp butter, softened
Salt and pepper to taste

Preheat outdoor grill at high heat and lightly oil grate.
Peel back corn husks and remove silk.
Place 1 tbsp butter, salt and pepper on each ear of corn; close husks.
Wrap each ear of corn tightly in aluminum foil.
Place on the prepared grill.
Cook approximately 30 minutes, turning occasionally, until corn is tender.

Serves 6

Lime Shrimp Kebabs

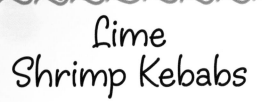

3 large limes
2 cloves garlic, finely chopped
¼ tsp black pepper
2 tsp olive oil
2 tbsp chopped fresh cilantro
16 large uncooked shrimp, peeled and deveined
8 small white button mushrooms
8 medium cherry tomatoes

Squeeze lime juice into a glass measuring cup. Add garlic, pepper, olive oil and cilantro and mix well.

Place the shrimp and mushrooms in a medium bowl and pour the cilantro/lime marinade over. Let marinate for 10 to 15 minutes in the refrigerator.

Preheat the broiler or light the grill. Drain the shrimp and mushrooms, reserving the marinade.

Thread, alternating, cherry tomatoes, mushrooms and shrimp on four skewers.

Grill kebabs over medium heat for 3 to 4 minutes on each side until the shrimp are no longer transparent. Baste the kebabs often during cooking with the reserved marinade.

Serves 4

Make kebabs by threading cherry tomatoes, mushrooms and shrimp on skewers.

Vegetable Garden

Veggie Kebabs with Very Garlicky Dressing

Very Garlicky Dressing

1 whole garlic bulb, top ½-inch cut off
1 ripe tomato
1 tbsp "Dijonnaise"
(creamy Dijon mustard blend)

2 drops Tabasco sauce
1 tsp Worcestershire sauce
1 tsp ground black pepper
½ cup olive oil

Preheat oven to 400° F.

In a baking pan, roast the garlic with the tomato for 30 minutes. (The tomato will shed its skin and the garlic will begin to ooze.)

Squeeze the garlic cloves, from their skin and place in the bowl of a food processor.

Coarsely chop the roasted tomato and add to food processor bowl.

Purée with the mustard, Tabasco sauce, Worcestershire sauce and pepper.

Slowly add olive oil until dressing is thick; set aside.

Veggie Kebabs

8 wooden skewers
½ green zucchini, cut into 1-inch chunks
½ yellow zucchini, cut into 1-inch chunks
8 cherry tomatoes
1 red onion, cut into 8 wedges

8 mushrooms, wiped clean
1 small orange bell pepper, seeded
   and cut into chunks
Olive oil for brushing

Soak wooden skewers in warm water for at least 10 minutes.

Divide the vegetables and thread on skewers, alternating to fit 2 of each vegetable on each skewer.

Brush with olive oil and grill or barbecue for 2 to 3 minutes per side.

Place cooked skewers on large serving platter and drizzle with Very Garlicky Dressing.

● ● ● ● ● ● ● ●

Makes 8 skewers

Barbecued Veggie Pockets

½ lb. new potatoes, thinly sliced
1 large red bell pepper, seeded and
cut into 1-inch pieces
1 large onion, sliced ¼-inch thick
5 oz. fresh green beans, cut into
1-inch pieces
1 sprig fresh rosemary
2 tbsp olive oil
1 tsp salt
1 tsp pepper
2 tbsp olive oil

● ● ● ● ● ● ● ● ●

Preheat grill at high heat.

In a large bowl, combine potatoes, red pepper, onion, green beans and rosemary. Stir in 2 tbsp olive oil and season with salt and pepper to coat.

Using 2 to 3 layers of aluminum foil, create desired number of foil packets.

Brush inside surfaces of packets with remaining olive oil. Distribute vegetables evenly among the packets; seal tightly.

Place packets on preheated grill.

Cook 30 minutes, turning once, or until potatoes are tender.

Serves 6

For many years we lived in a very hot and humid climate. Almost every yard in our neighborhood had a pool. This was not really a luxury but more of a necessity. Merely walking from your front door to your car door was like being in a sauna.

Every weekend a different household would host a pool party. Each guest would bring a dish for all to share. A buffet would be set up in the kitchen. As was customary, the kids would swim to their heart's content, while the adults sat around monitoring the pool activities and enjoying a visit. Our pool parties were the ideal way of making the best of a very hot, sticky season with the added pleasure of sharing some great dishes in good company.

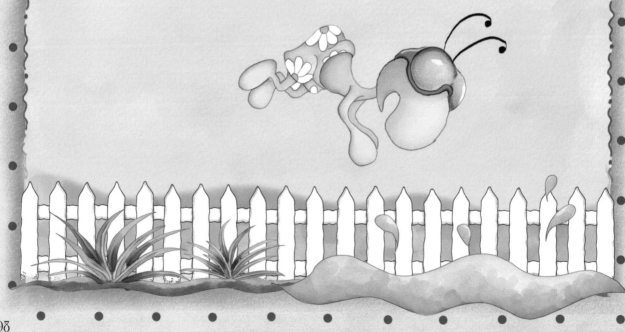

Pool Party

Sesame Chicken Strips

½ cup honey
⅓ cup sesame vinegar
½ cup water
¼ cup soy sauce
1 tbsp ketchup
2 tbsp cornstarch

3 cups cereal crumbs
(eg. corn flake crumbs)
¾ cup Parmesan cheese
¾ cup sesame seeds
½ cup buttermilk
2 eggs
3 lbs. chicken tenderloins

Sweet and Sour Sauce

Place the honey, vinegar, water, soy sauce, ketchup and cornstarch in a medium saucepan and bring to a boil. Stir continuously until the mixture has thickened. Refrigerate for at least 1 hour before using.

Chicken

Preheat oven to 350° F.

In a bowl, mix together the cereal crumbs, Parmesan cheese and sesame seeds.
In a separate bowl, whisk together buttermilk and eggs.
Rinse chicken tenders under running water; pat dry.
Dip the chicken in the buttermilk mixture, and then dredge with the bread crumb mixture to coat.
Place coated chicken strips in a shallow baking dish.
Bake for 20 to 30 minutes in the preheated oven.
Serve warm with Sweet and Sour Sauce, or let cool overnight and serve cold the next day.

Serves 10-12

Poolside Potato Salad

4 eggs
4 new potatoes
1 pint cherry or grape tomatoes
1 sweet bell pepper (yellow, red, or green),
seeded and cut into thin strips
1 small cucumber, sliced
2 heads lettuce, cut or torn into small pieces
1 small red onion, cut into thin rings
1 can tuna, drained
20 Kalamata olives (optional)

⅛ cup rice or balsamic vinegar
Rind of 1 lemon, grated
2 lemons, juiced
2 sprigs parsley, finely chopped
1 tbsp finely chopped mint
¼ tsp salt
½ tsp ground pepper
¼ cup olive oil

Salad

Cook eggs in boiling water for 10 minutes. Remove and place cooked eggs in a medium-sized bowl. Hold bowl under cold running water for a minute or two. Peel the shells from eggs and let cool on a clean cutting board.

Cook potatoes in fresh pot of boiling water until tender and skins are cracked, about 10 minutes. Remove from boiling water and let cool on a clean cutting board. Cut cooled eggs into quarters and place in a large bowl.

Add cherry tomatoes, bell pepper, cucumber, lettuce, onion, canned tuna, (and olives). Chop cooled potatoes into small chunks. Add to salad mixture.

Dressing

Place vinegar, lemon juice and rind, parsley, mint, salt and pepper in a small bowl. Whisk in olive oil.

Pour dressing over salad mixture and toss, coating evenly, using large serving spoons. Refrigerate for 30 minutes before serving.

Serves 4-6

Cool Cucumber Dip

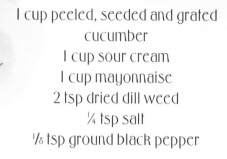

1 cup peeled, seeded and grated
cucumber
1 cup sour cream
1 cup mayonnaise
2 tsp dried dill weed
¼ tsp salt
⅛ tsp ground black pepper

In a medium bowl, mix together cucumber, sour cream,
mayonnaise, dill weed, salt and pepper. Cover and chill
in refrigerator for 8 hours, or overnight, before serving.

Serve with cucumber slices, carrot sticks and sliced bell peppers.

Makes about 2½ cups

Creamy Dill Dip

1 cup mayonnaise
2 tbsp finely chopped onions
1 tbsp finely chopped fresh dill
1 tbsp milk

In a small bowl, combine all ingredients, mixing well. Chill.
Serve with fresh vegetable pieces.

Makes 1 cup

Greek Pasta Salad

16-oz. pkg. bow-tie pasta
½ cup diced broccoli florets
½ cup diced cauliflower florets
15-oz. can black beans, drained
4-oz. can sliced black olives, drained
1 medium green bell pepper, seeded and diced
½ pint cherry tomatoes, halved
4 oz. crumbled feta cheese
1 cup Italian salad dressing
Salt and pepper to taste

Bring a large pot of lightly salted water to a boil. Add pasta and cook until tender, about 8 minutes.

Add broccoli and cauliflower florets to the boiling water during the last 5 minutes. Drain pasta and vegetables and run under cold water to cool.

In a large serving bowl, stir together the black beans, olives, green pepper, cherry tomatoes, feta cheese and Italian dressing.

Stir in the pasta, broccoli and cauliflower. Season with salt and pepper to taste.

Chill for at least 1 hour before serving.

Serves 10-12

Little Helper

Add cooked and cooled pasta, broccoli and cauliflower to salad.

Carrot and Raisin Salad

3 cups grated carrots
1 cup seedless raisins
1 tbsp honey
6 tbsp mayonnaise

¼ cup milk
1 tsp lemon juice
¼ tsp salt (optional)

In a large bowl, combine carrots and raisins, tossing lightly.
In a separate bowl, stir together remaining ingredients.
Pour mixture over carrots and raisins. Stir carefully until well combined.
Chill thoroughly before serving.

Serves 6-8

Strawberry Salad

2 small pkgs. strawberry Jell-O
1 cup boiling water
2 (10-oz.) pkgs. strawberries
1-lb.can crushed pineapple, drained
2 medium bananas, sliced
1 cup chopped nuts
1 pint sour cream

In a large bowl, dissolve Jell-O in boiling water. Fold in strawberries.
In a separate bowl, mix together pineapple, bananas and nuts. Fold into the gelatin mixture.
Pour half of mixture into casserole dish. Chill until firm. (Keep other half of mixture refrigerated.)
Spread sour cream over gelatin mixture in casserole dish. Top with remaining gelatin mixture. Chill until firm.

Serves 4-6

Fruit Pizza

18-oz. roll frozen sugar cookie dough
3-oz pkg. cream cheese, softened
⅓ cup sugar
1 tsp vanilla
¾ cup chilled whipping cream
Assorted fresh fruits:
      strawberry halves
      grapes
      blueberries
      peach slices
      raspberries
      banana slices
½ cup apricot preserves
1 tbsp water

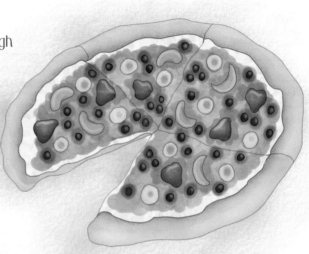

Preheat oven according to cookie dough package directions.
Slice cookie dough into ¼-inch slices.
Place side by side in a round pizza pan.
Bake, following directions on package. Let cool completely.

In a small mixing bowl, beat together cream cheese, sugar and vanilla on low speed until smooth.
Add whipping cream to mixture and beat on medium speed until stiff peaks form.
Spread over cookie crust.
Arrange fruits decoratively on top.
In a small saucepan, over very low heat, make a glaze by heating apricot preserves and water. Brush glaze over fruit.
Refrigerate for at least 2 hours.

Serves 8-10

Note: Will not keep well for very long.
Enjoy now!

Waldorf Salad

¾ cup chopped pecans
3 medium-sized tart green apples,
   cored and cut into chunks
3 tbsp lemon juice
1 stalk celery, minced
2 cups seedless green grapes, halved
1 cup diced Cheddar cheese

Dressing
1 cup plain yogurt
¼ cup mayonnaise
½ cup orange juice
Rind of ½ orange, grated
(optional)

Toast pecans under grill until lightly browned, about 3-5 minutes, watching carefully that they not burn.

Prepare all salad ingredients and toss together in a large bowl.

In a small bowl, whisk together dressing ingredients. Pour over salad and mix well to coat.

Serves 4-6

Mandarin Orange Salad

1 small carton cottage cheese
1 large pkg. orange Jello-O
1 medium can crushed pineapple, drained
1 can mandarin oranges, drained
12-oz carton whipped topping

In a large bowl, lightly mix together the cottage cheese and Jell-O. Gently stir in the pineapple and oranges. Fold in the whipped topping. Chill until firm.

Serves 4-6

Mexican Taco Dip

16-oz. container sour cream
8-oz. pkg. cream cheese, softened
1-oz. pkg. taco seasoning mix
16-oz. pkg. shredded Cheddar cheese
16-oz. jar prepared salsa
1 cup shredded lettuce
1 tomato, cubed
2 green onions, sliced
1-lb. bag corn tortilla chips

In a large bowl, mix together the sour cream, cream cheese and taco seasoning mix. Spread the mixture into a medium serving dish.
Layer the sour cream mixture with Cheddar cheese, salsa and lettuce. Top with tomato and green onions. Serve with corn tortilla chips for dipping.

Serves 12-24

Fresh Fruit Salsa

½ red onion, finely chopped
1 mango, diced
1 cup diced watermelon
¼ cup finely chopped cilantro
1 tbsp lime juice
½ tbsp olive oil
2 oranges, sectioned, chopped and seeds removed
1 grapefruit, sectioned, chopped and seeds removed

Combine all ingredients in a bowl.
Cover and chill for at least 1 hour before serving.
Serve with grilled fish, chicken, or any Mexican meal.

Serves 8

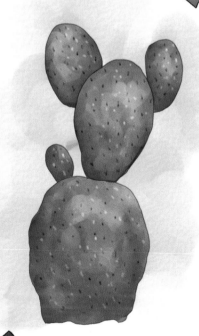

Cinnamon Apple Salad

3-oz pkg. lemon-flavored gelatin
¼ cup red cinnamon candies
I cup boiling water
I cup unsweetened applesauce
½ tbsp lemon juice
⅓ tsp salt
¼ cup chopped nuts
I cup cottage cheese

In a bowl, dissolve gelatin and red cinnamon candies in boiling water. Stir in applesauce, lemon juice and dash of salt. Chill until partially set.
Stir in nuts and pour into 8x8x2-inch pan.
Blend cottage cheese in electric blender until smooth.
Spread cottage cheese on top of gelatin and swirl cottage cheese through salad just enough to obtain a marble effect.
Chill until firm.

Serves 4-5

Blueberry Surprise

2 small boxes Jell-O (any berry flavor)
2 cups boiling water
2 small cans crushed pineapple, drained
I can blueberry pie filling

Topping
8 oz. cream cheese
½ cup sour cream
½ cup sugar
I tsp vanilla
½ cup pecan pieces

In a large bowl, dissolve Jell-O in boiling water.
Stir in the pineapple and blueberry pie filling, blending well. Chill.
In a separate bowl, mix together topping ingredients and spread over chilled gelatin. Chill.

Serves 8-10

Shrimp Salad

2 cups cooked shrimp
  (peeled and deveined)
1 cup finely chopped celery
1 tbsp finely minced onion
1 tbsp fresh lemon juice
½ cup mayonnaise
Salt and pepper to taste
Romaine lettuce or iceberg lettuce
Thinly sliced tomatoes
Avocado slices, cherry tomatoes (optional)

In a large bowl, mix together shrimp,
celery, onion, lemon juice, mayonnaise, salt and pepper.

Arrange lettuce leaves on serving plates; top with thinly sliced tomatoes.

Spoon shrimp mixture over lettuce and tomatoes. Garnish with avocado slices or cherry tomatoes, if desired.

Serves 4

Prepare serving plates by arranging them with lettuce leaves and tomato slices.

WaterMelon Fruit Dip

1-2 apples, cored and sliced
½ cantaloupe or honeydew melon,
cut into spears
1 pint strawberries
½ fresh pineapple, cut into chunks

Dip
2 cups chunks seedless watermelon
10-oz. pkg. frozen raspberries,
defrosted
½ cup fruit-flavored softened cream
cheese
1 cup Balkan-style yogurt
2 tsp lemon juice

Arrange cut fruit on a large serving plate. Cover with plastic wrap to reduce browning and refrigerate until ready to serve.
Place 2 cups watermelon chunks, raspberries and cream cheese in a blender or food processor. Purée until smooth. Transfer into a bowl.
Stir in yogurt and lemon juice. Whisk until mixed well.
Pour the dip into one or more serving bowls.
Arrange fruit around dip bowls, or on a separate plate to serve.

Serves 10-12

Millionaire Fluff

1 cup coconut
9-oz. can pineapple tidbits, well drained
1 cup miniature marshmallows
4½ oz. whipped topping
¼ cup chopped cherries
½ cup pecan pieces
3 tbsp milk

In a large bowl, mix together all ingredients.
Chill until set.

Serves 4-6

Poolside Party Mix

6 tbsp butter
2 tbsp Worcestershire sauce
¾ tsp garlic powder
1½ tsp seasoning salt
½ tsp onion powder
I cup peanuts
I cup mini pretzels
3 cups crispy corn cereal squares
3 cups crispy wheat cereal squares
1½ cups candy-coated chocolate pieces
1½ cups raisins

Preheat oven to 250° F.

Melt butter in a 9x13-inch baking pan.

Remove baking pan from oven. Stir in the Worcestershire sauce, garlic powder, seasoning salt and onion powder.

Gradually mix in the peanuts, pretzels, crispy corn cereal and crispy wheat cereal. Toss to evenly coat all ingredients.

Bake approximately I hour in the preheated oven. Let cool.

Mix in chocolate candies and raisins.

Store the mixture in a tightly-covered container until ready to serve.

Serves 24

Little Helper

Add chocolate candies and raisins to cooled mixture; stir to mix.

Banana Pops

4 ripe bananas, peeled
8 wooden popsicle sticks
6-oz. pkg. semi-sweet or milk
chocolate morsels
1 tbsp shortening
Chopped nuts (optional)
Shredded coconut (optional)

Cut bananas in half crosswise. Insert a wooden popsicle stick in end of each.
Freeze.
In a double boiler, melt morsels over hot (not boiling) water; stir in shortening.
Coat each frozen banana half with chocolate mixture.
Carefully roll in nuts or coconut, if desired.
Wrap each pop in aluminum foil, or put in freezer bags and store in freezer.

Makes 8 pops

Chocolate Creamsicle Pie

8-oz. pkg. fat-free cream cheese, softened
16-oz. container frozen non-dairy dessert
    topping (Cool Whip), thawed
1 cup vanilla yogurt
1 cup orange juice
1 packet sugar-free orange Jell-o
2 chocolate cookie pie crusts (prepared)

In a large bowl, combine cream cheese with thawed dessert topping; blend until
creamy. Add yogurt and orange juice; blend with mixer until very creamy.
Sprinkle in Jell-O; stir until well blended. Spoon evenly into two pie crusts.
Chill several hours before serving.

Serves 16

Giant Ice Cream Sandwich

15-oz. pkg. fudge brownie mix
⅔ cup water
½ cup vegetable oil
2 eggs
1 cup semi-sweet chocolate chips
8 cups vanilla ice cream, slightly softened

Topping
2 cups icing sugar
⅔ cup semi-sweet chocolate chips
1 cup evaporated milk
½ cup margarine or butter
1 tsp vanilla

Preheat oven to 350° F. Line two 12-inch round pizza pans with foil.

In large bowl, combine brownie mix, water, oil, eggs and 1 cup chocolate chips; mix well. Spread half of batter in each foil-lined pan. Bake for 15 to 20 minutes. (Do not over bake). Cool. Freeze 1 to 2 hours for ease in handling. Remove from pans; remove foil.

To assemble: place 1 brownie round on serving plate. Spoon softened ice cream evenly over brownie. Top with remaining brownie. Cover and freeze until firm. Meanwhile, in medium saucepan, combine sugar, ⅔ cup chocolate chips, milk and margarine. Bring to a boil; cook 8 minutes, stirring constantly. Remove from heat and stir in vanilla. Cool.

Let ice cream sandwich stand at room temperature for 10 to 15 minutes before serving. Cut into wedges and drizzle with topping.

Serves 8-10

Poolside Peach Slush

1 cup milk
2 cups sliced peaches
(fresh or canned)
2 tsp sugar

Pour milk into ice cube trays and freeze until solid, 1-2 hours.
Pop the milk cubes out of the tray and place in a blender.
Add peaches and sugar to blender.
Blend on high speed until everything is well mixed together and very smooth.
Pour into small cups and serve right away.

Serves 6

Pineapple Lemonade

4 cups crushed ice
1 quart sparkling water, chilled
½ cup sugar
3 cups pineapple juice
½ cup lemon juice
1 lemon, sliced

Divide ice and sparkling water among 4 tall glasses.
Mix sugar, pineapple juice and lemon juice in a blender, on high speed, until smooth.
Pour over ice and sparkling water in glasses.
Garnish with lemon slices.

Serves 4

Strawberry Milk Frost

1 cup fresh or frozen strawberries,
thawed and drained
1 cup milk
2 tbsp sugar
1 tsp vanilla
1 cup vanilla ice cream, softened
Fresh strawberries for garnish

Place 1 cup strawberries and half the milk in a blender; blend
until strawberries are puréed.
Add remaining milk, sugar and vanilla; blend until well
combined. Add ice cream and blend until frothy.
Serve in tall glasses topped with fresh strawberries.

Serves 3-4

Hawaiian Delight Soda

¾ cup fruit punch
2 scoops pineapple sherbet
¾ cup lemon-lime soda
Whipped cream
Pineapple chunks
Maraschino cherries

Pour punch into a tall glass.
Add sherbet and soda. Stir well.
Top with whipped cream, pineapple
chunks and a cherry.

Serves 1-2

INDEX

Index

Index

METRIC CONVERSION GUIDE

Volume

⅛ tsp = 0.5 ml
¼ tsp = 1 ml
½ tsp = 2 ml
¾ tsp = 3 ml
1 tsp = 5 ml
1 tbsp = 15 ml
¼ cup = 50 ml
⅓ cup = 75 ml
½ cup = 125 ml
⅔ cup = 150 ml

¾ cup = 175 ml
1 cup = 250 ml
(2 cups = 1 pint)
(4 cups = 1 quart)
1 quart = 1 liter
1 fluid ounce (2 tbsp) = 30 ml
4 fluid ounces (½ cup) = 125 ml
8 fluid ounces (1 cup) = 250 ml
12 fluid ounces (1½ cups) = 375 ml
16 fluid ounces (2 cups) = 500 ml

Weight

1 ounce =30 grams
16 ounces = 1 pound = 450 grams
¼ lb. = 115 grams
½ lb. = 225 grams
¾ lb. = 350 grams
1 lb. = 450 grams
2.2 lbs. = 1 kilogram

Measurements

1 inch = 2.5 centimeters
1 foot = 30 centimeters
39 inches = 1 meter
⅛ inch = 3 mm
¼ inch = 6 mm
½ inch = 1.3 cm

Temperatures

200º F = 100º C
250º F = 120º C
275º F = 140º C
300º F = 150º C
325º F = 160º C
350º F = 180º C
375º F = 190º C
400º F = 200º C
425º F = 220º C
450º F = 230º C